Tax Guide 103

FAMILY
TAX
STRATEGIES

by

Holmes F. Crouch
Tax Specialist

Published by

Allyear Tax Guides

20484 Glen Brae Drive
Saratoga, CA 95070

343.705
C

ISBN 0-944817-68-8

LCCN 2003108855

Printed in U.S.A.

Series 100
Individuals & Families

Tax Guide 103

FAMILY TAX STRATEGIES

[2nd Edition]

For other titles in print, see page 224.

The author: **Holmes F. Crouch**
For more about the author, see page 221.

PREFACE

If you are a knowledge-seeking **taxpayer** looking for information, this book can be helpful to you. It is designed to be read — from cover to cover — in about eight hours. Or, it can be "skim-read" in about 30 minutes.

Either way, you are treated to **tax knowledge** . . . *beyond the ordinary*. The "beyond" is that which cannot be found in IRS publications, FedWorld on-line services, tax software programs, Internet chatrooms, or e-mail bulletins.

Taxpayers have different levels of interest in a selected subject. For this reason, this book starts with introductory fundamentals and progresses onward. You can verify the progression by chapter and section in the table of contents. In the text, "applicable law" is quoted in pertinent part. Key phrases and key tax forms are emphasized. Real-life examples are given . . . in down-to-earth style.

This book has 12 chapters. This number provides depth without cross-subject rambling. Each chapter starts with a head summary of meaningful information.

To aid in your skim-reading, informative diagrams and tables are placed strategically throughout the text. By leafing through page by page, reading the summaries and section headings, and glancing at the diagrams and tables, you can get a good handle on the matters covered.

Effort has been made to update and incorporate all of the latest tax law changes that are *significant* to the title subject. However, "beyond the ordinary" does not encompass every conceivable variant of fact and law that might give rise to protracted dispute and litigation. Consequently, if a particular statement or paragraph is crucial to your own specific case, you are urged to seek professional counseling. Otherwise, the information presented is general and is designed for a broad range of reader interests.

The Author

INTRODUCTION

The term "family," as we use it here, implies one or more parents, one or more children, and one or more grandparents. The idea of a family is that at least one member of each of three generations is living at the same time. The reason for focusing on three generations is that the Internal Revenue Code applies to all living individuals from birth to death. As such, the taxation of income, gifts, and inheritances produces intra-family linkages down through generational lines. It is this "tax circle" from birth to death that makes family tax strategizing so important.

Our approach is to first familiarize you with the *anatomy* of an income tax return. Yes, a tax return, Form 1040 particularly, has anatomical body parts of its own. These parts consist of filing status, exemptions for dependents, gross income (15 sources), adjustments to gross (11 items), personal deductions, regular tax, nonrefundable credits (14 potential), other taxes (6 possible), and, finally, the total tax. Human nature is such that one always seeks to minimize his total tax for a given year. Hence, our underlying goal is to put human nature to work.

For more than 75 years, the conventional wisdom was to transfer income-producing assets from senior members of a family (who were in higher tax brackets) to junior members of the family (who were in lower tax brackets). This is still good wisdom for tax strategizing. But, today, there's a BIG difference. When such assets are transferred to a child under age 14, the tax rate automatically jumps to that of the parent. Instead of a 10% rate, for example, the child pays at an up-to-35% rate. Thus, today, it is more prudent to take advantage of the many tax-offsetting opportunities that Congress has provided.

New tax reduction opportunities for families keep cropping up all the time. Within the past few years alone, Congress has been directing more of its benevolence towards families with children, and the need to pay for higher education. This is the domain of deductions for student loan interest, tuition and fees, maintaining and improving skills in one's employment, plus education, child, and adoption credits. We offer specific guidance on these items, as well as quoting the pertinent tax laws thereon.

For example, for children under age 17, the child tax credit has been increased from $600 to $1,000 but most of the credit is lost where the parents' combined income exceeds $110,000. Also, the child adoption credit has increased from $5,000 to $10,000 PER CHILD (**not** per year). There is no limit to the number of children that a couple can adopt. By far, the greatest "family friendly" changes pertain to education tax credits and other educational tax incentives. Where an employer provides financial assistance towards continuing education, up to $5,250 of that assistance is excluded entirely from the taxable income of the employee student.

Our primary strategy focuses on **multiple filings**. The idea is to maximize the number of tax returns being filed in a family. The greater the number of tax returns filed, the more diluted the total family tax becomes. The multiple filers are single persons over the age of 14, children working part-time up to the age of 19, full-time students (5 months of the year) up to age 24, young marrieds of any age (who have no dependents of their own), and elderly parents who have difficulty comprehending the tax laws.

Another strategy focuses on **gratuitous transfers** (gifts, inheritances, and gift-type "loans") from grandparents or from middle-aged and elderly members in the overall family structure. The idea here is to dilute the death tax consequences of those family members who are blessed with modest wealth. Simultaneously, each transferor is assured that throughout his senile years, his income tax returns will be properly filed. This creates a new dependency status which we call "dependents in fact." These are older family members who require no or negligible money support from the primary filer. Still, they are dependent upon the primary filer for tax advice, supervision, and follow-through in the preparation and filing of their own returns.

Most persons will file income tax returns over a 35- to 50-year period of their lifetimes. Some will file over longer periods: **up to 70 years** (from age 15 or younger through age 85 or older). This is the background of reality that we want you to keep in mind, as we progress throughout this book.

CONTENTS

Chapter	Page

1

FILING STATUS CHOICES

The Filing Status Checkboxes On Form 1040 Are: (1) Single, (2) Married/Joint, (3) Married/Separate, (4) Head Of Household, And (5) Qualifying Widow(er). Each Becomes An ENTRY POINT Into Federal Tax Rate Schedules. Multiple Checkboxes Can Be Used Where There Are Multiple Filings By Those Dependents Who Are Claimed By The Filing Parent(s). Dependents Who Are Employed Can Use Form 1040EZ; Those With Interest And Dividends Over $400 (Or Retired: Such As Grandparents) Can Use Form 1040A; Those Dependents Who Are Self-Employed Or Have Capital Gain Must Use Form 1040. Parents Also Must Use Form 1040.

One factor when strategizing for best family tax benefits is to check the proper filing status. If you recall, or if you will take a moment to look at Form 1040, you will note that, just below your name and address block, there is a *Filing Status* block. It consists of five checkboxes. Just below the heading "filing status" in the left-hand white space, a small-print instruction says—

Check only one box.

Implicitly, this instruction also means: check only the correct box.

Depending on the numerical size of your family, and its age and occupational diversity, you can check more than one box. To do so, however, more than one tax return (for a given year) needs to be filed. The "only one box" instruction applies to one tax return at a time. There is nothing improper about filing multiple returns by different family members, using the same family address.

To illustrate our point, suppose you are a parent who is earning a comfortable income. You are financially able to support a school-age son *and* a retirement-age mother. Your son works part-time and earns some money. Your mother collects a modest retirement income. Your son and your mother can each file a return on his/her own. Even so, you can still claim each as a dependent on your return . . . if the proper conditions are met.

In this, our introductory chapter, we want to familiarize you with the different filing status choices that may — or can — apply to your particular family situation. The proper choice of filing status sets the stage for the tax rates that apply. You cannot pick, arbitrarily, a filing status that will give you the lowest tax. You have to claim that status that corresponds to your state of marriage, divorce, death, unemployment, and the dependents, if any, that you have. If you truly understand the role of filing status in your tax return preparations, you can use family changes over the years to your distinct tax advantage.

The Checkboxes: Five

As mentioned, there are five filing status checkboxes. You have seen them before, but probably never really thought about them in depth. They are displayed quite prominently in the head portion of Form 1040. This form is officially titled: *U.S. Individual Income Tax Return*. This title implies very clearly that Form 1040 applies only to individuals and their families.

There are other forms in the "1040 series." There is Form 1040A (a "short form" 1040), Form 1040-C (departing alien), Form 1040-ES (estimated tax), Form 1040EZ (single filer, no dependents), Form 1040NR (nonresident alien), Form 1040-PR (Puerto Rico), Form 1040-SS (Virgin Islands, Guam, American Samoa, and Northern Mariana Islands), Form 1040-TEL (single telefiler), Form 1040-V (payment voucher), and Form 1040-X (amended return).

For better presentation focus, we will limit our discussion to Forms 1040, 1040A, and 1040EZ. Form 1040 is treated as the principal family return, with **all** dependents listed thereon. The "A" and "EZ" versions are supplemental forms for those dependents who have modest amounts of income on their own, while remaining as dependents on the primary 1040. All other variants in the 1040 series are special purpose forms for which filing status choices are quite restricted. For our purposes, we present in Figure 1.1 an overview of the multiple filings possible.

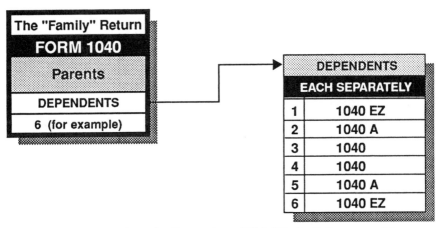

Fig. 1.1 - Potential Filings for Dependents With (Modest) Sources of Income

The five filing-status checkboxes are:

1. ☐ *Single*

2. ☐ *Married Filing Jointly*

3. ☐ *Married Filing Separately*

4. ☐ *Head of Household*

5. ☐ *Qualifying Widow(er)*

Of these five, the only one that displays no additional wording on Form 1040 is Box 1: "single." All four other boxes carry specific qualifying words to alert you to the restrictions that apply.

For Box 2, "married filing jointly," for example, the qualifying words are—

> . . . *even if only one* [spouse] *had* [the] *income.*

For Box 3, "married filing separately," the qualifying words are—

> *Enter spouse's social security number above and full name here*
> ▶ _____.

In the case of Box 4 and Box 5, there are other qualifying conditions where a current spouse is not involved. Box 4, "head of household," includes the wording—

> . . . *with qualifying person. If the qualifying person is a child but not your dependent, enter this child's name here* ▶ _____
> _____.

Similarly, Box 5, "qualifying widow(er)," includes the wording—

> . . . *with dependent child (year spouse died* ▶ _____).

It is — or should be — self-evident from the 5-box listing above, that Form 1040 is a family-oriented tax return form. Four of the five selection boxes are clearly applicable to spousal and dependent situations. So, too, is "single" status, as you'll see shortly below.

Tax Rate Dependency

Why is the correct selection of filing status so important?

Answer: It determines the "entry point" into federal tax tables and tax rate schedules. Each table and each schedule has a different tax rate structure. Obviously, if your entry point into the tax rate structure is incorrect, the final tax that you ascertain is also incorrect.

The difference between a tax table and a tax rate schedule is the amount of **taxable income** that you end up with on your return. You use the **tax tables** when your taxable income is *less than*

$100,000. When your taxable income reaches or exceeds $100,000, the **tax rate schedules** must be used. There is no limit to the amount of income that the schedules can handle. However, the tax rates "flatten out" — at around 38% — for incomes over $300,000. This taxable income range pretty well covers all family situations where strategizing for the lowest tax is a worthwhile endeavor.

How are the filing status entry points designated on the tables and schedules?

Unlike the five filing status boxes, there are only *four* tax tables/schedules. One of the tables/schedules serves "double duty." Married filing jointly doubles for qualifying widow(er).

The tables/schedules direct you to the correct rate structure with the following lead-in instructions—

Tax Tables

If your taxable income is . . . at least $_____ . . . but less than $_____, and you are—

- *Single*
- *Married filing jointly (also qualifying widow(er))*
- *Married filing separately*
- *Head of household*

Tax Rate Schedules

If your taxable income is . . . over $_____ . . . but not over $_____, use . . .

- *Schedule X   — Single*
- *Schedule Y-1   — Married filing jointly or qualifying widow(er)*
- *Schedule Y-2   — Married filing separately*
- *Schedule Z   — Head of household*

To illustrate the different tax results from different filing status entries, we present Figure 1.2. Note that we start the information in that figure at $25,000 as taxable income. Each income level shown

Taxable	Federal Filing Status			
Income	Single	Married Joint	Married Separate	Head of Household
25,000	3,450	3,150	3,450	3,250
50,000	9,850	7,290	10,400	8,710
75,000	16,810	14,050	17,700	15,250
100,000	24,310	20,800	25,910	22,100
125,000	31,800	27,900	34,650	29,600
150,000	39,750	35,400	43,400	37,100
175,000	48,500	43,100	52,930	45,500
200,000	57,250	51,810	62,580	54,270
225,000	66,000	60,560	72,220	63,020
250,000	74,750	69,300	81,880	71,770

NOTE: Amounts are "rounded" and are based on 2002 Tax Rate Schedules

Fig. 1.2 - Example Tax Amounts for Filing Status Taxable Incomes

applies across the board, separately, to each filing status. We display the tax result differences at increments of $25,000 up to $250,000. In all cases, for the **same taxable income**, married filing jointly gives the lowest tax. Married filing separately gives the highest tax. The difference between the lowest and highest tax (in Figure 1.2) increases markedly as the taxable income increases.

At $25,000, for example, the difference (married separate minus married joint) is $300. At $125,000 the difference is $6,750; at $250,000 it is $12,580. Consequently, the filing status tax differences become increasingly important as one's family taxable income increases. With this realization in mind, a useful strategizing objective evolves. That is, where there are multiple family members, and where it is proper to do so, the filing of *multiple* tax returns (for a given year) can be highly beneficial.

Multiple Uses of "Single"

A "family" consists of one or more parents, one or more children, and one or more grandparents. When the parents file jointly or separately, claiming one or more dependents, there are opportunities for the children and grandparents to each file as a single person. If they do so legitimately, there is a "tax dilution" benefit to the family income overall. Let us explain.

The instructions to Form 1040 say that one may check the single box if *any* of the following conditions exist for the taxable year:

- Never married, or
- Legally separated, or
- Widowed.

The "never married" status would apply to minor children, particularly, and to older children who are unmarried. The "widowed" status would apply to a grandparent on the children's father's side *and* to a grandparent on the children's mother's side. The "legally separate" status would apply to the parents themselves under a decree of divorce or of separate maintenance (under state law where the parents reside).

The real tipoff as to what can take place is found in the small-print instruction at Box 6a on Form 1040. This box — 6a — follows immediately below Box 5 in the filing status section. Box 6a is labeled:

☐ *Yourself*

This designation is immediately followed by:

*If your parent (or someone else) can claim you as a dependent on his or her tax return, **do not** check this box.*

The "yourself instruction" carries an implicitly clear message. Parents, either filing jointly or separately, can claim all unmarried children and all widowed grandparents as dependents on the parents' returns. Parents can do this, irrespective of the income of the children and grandparents. In most family situations, the parents are in a higher tax bracket than their dependent children and grandparents. Whereas parents of ordinary means (middle and upper-middle income) could be in the 25%, 30%, or 35% brackets, children and grandparents would almost invariably be in the 10% to 15% tax brackets. For single filers, the 15% bracket extends up to about $25,000 of taxable income. For family pooled-income arrangements, multiple filing of single returns is the way to go.

Let us pose a strictly hypothetical example. A family consists of two living parents, two unmarried children, and two widowed grandparents. The pooled income of the family is $100,000 taxable. The "married filing jointly" tax on this amount is $20,800.

Suppose each single filer (there are four), had a taxable income of $10,000. (Remember, this all hypothetical; you'll see the weaknesses in Chapter 2.) The tax for each would be $1,200 [10% x $6,000 + 15% x $4,000] . When the $40,000 income of the four single filers is removed from the family income pool, the parents' taxable amount reduces to $60,000 [$100,000 − 40,000]. At this point the parents' tax becomes $10,000 (approximately). Add $4,800 (4 x $1,200 for each single filer) and the result is $14,800. This is a family tax **saving** of $6,000 [$20,800 − 14,800], provided each single filer does not claim for himself an exemption.

Variations of "Married" Status

Ordinarily, one is married if he is legally married under state law where he and his spouse reside. For any given taxable year, the legality of marriage is determined *at the close* of the taxable year. Thus, technically, if a couple gets married at 3:00 p.m. on December 31, they are treated for tax purposes as married for the entire year. Conversely, if a couple gets divorced at 3:00 p.m. on December 31, they are tax treated as though they were unmarried for the entire year. This tax treatment opens up a range of variations in marital status. The consequence is that federal tax law and state family law **do not coincide** on a day-by-day basis.

The specific tax law on point is Section 7703: *Determination of Marital Status*. Its general rule, subsection (a) reads—

(1) The determination of whether an individual is married shall be made as of the close of his taxable year; except that if his spouse dies during [the] *year, such determination shall be made as of the time of such death.*

(2) An individual legally separated from his spouse under a decree of divorce or of separate maintenance, shall not be considered as married.

Section 7703(b) addresses: *Certain Married Individuals Living Apart.* The "living apart" aspect is where one spouse furnishes more than one-half of the cost of *maintaining a household* for more than one-half of the taxable year . . . for a dependent child, parent, or other relative. Under these circumstances, Section 7703(b) reads—

An individual who is married . . . and who files a separate return [while maintaining a principal place of abode for a dependent] *and during the last 6 months of the taxable year, such individual's spouse is* **not** *a member of such household, such individual shall not be considered as married.*

Section 7703(b) is called the "deemed unmarried" rule. It is federal tax recognition of the fact that parents may, indeed, live apart — for whatever reason. Such fact may exist irrespective of whether or not a decree of divorce or separate maintenance is in effect. We are dealing here with federal law: not state law. When a parent is deemed unmarried, his/her proper filing status is either single with a dependent or head of household. Married filing jointly does not apply.

The only unmarried situation where married filing jointly applies is a qualifying widow(er). The qualification required is that there be a dependent child, and that the spouses could have filed jointly for the year of death. Additionally, the surviving parent must not have remarried during the following two years.

Married filing jointly does not apply where—

. . . *either the husband or wife* **at any time** *during the taxable year is a* **nonresident alien** [Sec. 6013(a)(1)].

However, Section 6013(g) permits filing jointly where the alien spouse **elects** to be treated as a U.S. resident. If such an election is made, the married joint income includes the worldwide income of the alien spouse.

In Figure 1.3 we summarize the filing status options for parents who are not legally divorced or separated (under state law). As is illustrated, there is quite a range of filing status choices where there are dependent children, grandparents, or other relatives. As our national economy becomes more globalized, nontraditional family tax situations will arise.

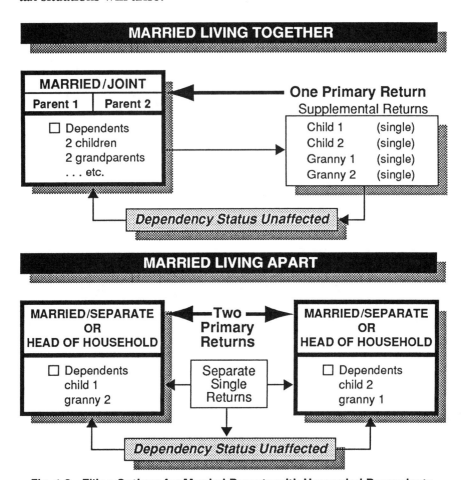

Fig. 1.3 - Filing Options for Married Parents with Unmarried Dependents

Married Filing Separately

Married filing separately is always an option. This is so, whether the spouses as parents live together or live separately. Filing separately is often done strictly for occupational and financial reasons. The husband earns $150,000 where the wife earns

$50,000, for example. The wife's $50,000 is derived from her inherited property. She wants to keep her inherited money separate from the marital money in order to pass it on — someday — to her children. Married filing separately is one way to keep the parental accounting strictly separate. This is especially desirable where the parents are remarried, after having been divorced or widowed from prior spouses. Separate returns may also be indicated where the parents are preparing for divorce, and physically live apart from each other.

Technically speaking, for the same total family income split 50/50 — or nearly so — the tax is the same whether married filing jointly, or *two* marrieds filing separately. Suppose, for example, the total taxable income is $100,000 split 50/50 between the spousal parents. At $100,000 taxable, the tax is $20,800 for married/jointly (using Figure 1.2 for 2002). At $50,000 taxable, the tax is $10,400 for one married/separate return. For two married/separate returns, the tax would be $20,800 (10,400 + 10,400). Thus, if the family income and deductions are more or less divided equally, there is nil difference in the tax consequences.

When there is a non-50/50 split of the income and deductions between parent (H) ["H" for husband] and parent (W) ["W" for wife], the tax disparity between married/joint and married/separate widens. For example, suppose parent (H) reports a taxable income of $100,000 and parent (W) reports $50,000. The two married/separate taxes would be $25,910 and $10,400, for a total of $36,310 (from Figure 1.2). If filed as married/joint, the tax would be $35,400. If parent (H) reports $150,000 taxable and parent (W) continues with $50,000 taxable, the two married/separates total $53,800 (43,400 + 10,400). The corresponding married/joint tax would be $51,810 (at $200,000 taxable). Check these figures and other splits of your choice by referring to Figure 1.2.

We present the comparative tax amounts above for a particular reason. From the point of view of family strategizing for reduction of taxes, married filing *separately* should **not** be your first choice. It should be your last such choice. You checkbox the married/separate status as a default procedure. You do so when there is no other effective tax way to preserve clear-cut separation of financial records by determined spouses.

Head-of-Household Status

Head of household is truly a unique filing status. It applies to *unmarried* individuals who provide a home for one or more dependent children, grandparents, or other relatives. Specifically, the term "unmarried" applies only to those persons who are legally separated from their spouses under a decree of divorce or separate maintenance. However, the term also includes parents who are "deemed unmarried" by virtue of their living apart for the last six months or more of any taxable year.

Aside from being unmarried or deemed unmarried, the key qualification of a head-of-household filer is that he or she **maintain a home** for one or more qualifying persons. "Maintaining a home" means paying more than half of the cost of keeping it up, and paying more than half of the cost of supporting the dependent. Ordinarily, a qualified dependent must live in your home more than half of the year. If your child lives at school, it is considered as living at home. This is because the home (which you maintain) is the "place of return" for a child at school.

Where there is a child or children, and the parents live apart, the parent maintaining a household for one or more children can claim head-of-household status, even when the other parent claims one or more as dependents. This separation of filing status and dependency status is clearly implied in the preprinted instruction at Box 4 on Form 1040. Said box (again) reads:

If a qualifying person is a child but not your dependent, enter this child's name here. ▶ _____

We'll have more on dependency qualifications in Chapter 2: Dependents & Exemptions.

For living apart (deemed unmarried) parents, two heads of household can be used. This applies where two or more dependents are involved. The parents can agree among themselves (on a year-to-year basis) as to which dependent(s) each will claim. To do so, however, each must maintain a separate home which is the principal place of domicile of one or more qualifying dependents. For your convenience, we present a summary of the head-of-household filing status in Figure 1.4. In those situations where the marriage is turbulent, the strategic use of head-of-household status can restore tax sanity to both parents.

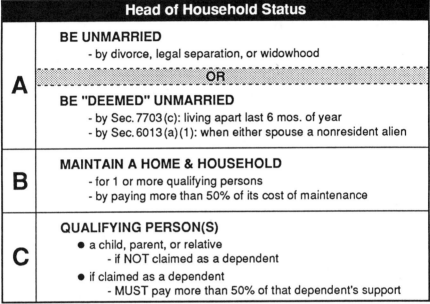

Fig. 1.4 - Basic Requirements for Head of Household Status

Head-of-Household Versatility

In the U.S. today, marriages, divorces, separations, and remarriages are common social, economic, and family realities. Let's skip over divorce situations and stick to the basic premise of two parents (with children and grandparents) simply living apart. As is so often the case, they have "grown apart" for various nonscandalous reasons. There are conflicts in job demands; he travels a lot; she works early or late. They differ markedly on the treatment and guidance of children, especially during teenage years. They handle money differently: one parent is a spendthrift; the other is a pennypincher. When grandparents live in, there can be "in-law" controversies. When the children go off to college, or take to living on their own, there are different parental concerns about their lifestyles, their food and drink habits, the peer pressures, and the ease of procuring drugs and guns. Unless either parent has a new spouse in mind, the separate parents live apart simply because there is less hassle in doing so. They remain as true friends and spouses. They do so for the sake of family stability and more harmonious relations. Often, the plan is to reunite, once all children are on their own and all grandparents are deceased.

To illustrate the versatility of head-of-household status, let us assume that there are two or more children and two or more grandparents in the family unit. By mutual agreement (or by legal separation decree), the live-apart parents might choose as follows:

Parent (H) — husband
- child 1   (youngest)
- child 3
- grandparent 2   (oldest)

Parent (W) — wife
- child 2   (youngest)
- grandparent 1
- grandparent 3   (oldest)

Note that for each of the two parents we list the youngest dependent first. As the older dependents become of legal age, or become deceased, they "disappear" from the tax return of the claiming parent. For tax authority computer-matching purposes, a fixed arrangement of dependents provides an element of consistency from year to year.

Even though the dependency listing arrangement on each parent's tax return is fixed, there is nothing to prevent the "switching of dependents" back and forth, as family conditions warrant. This is effective so long as each parent maintains his/her initially agreed number of dependents. For example, child 3 may be switched for grandparent 3. It may be that child 3 prefers living temporarily with parent (W) because of that parent's proximity to sports, educational, and recreational facilities. Grandparent 3 may be starting to fail fast and be in need of major or long-term medical attention, which parent (H) can better afford. Thus, when separated parents remain as friends, two heads-of-household are near ideal.

It could be that at some point one parent's dependents all disappear from his/her tax return. In such event, that parent becomes a single filer. If the legally married parents continue to live apart, the single status of one does not affect the head-of-household status of the other (who continues to maintain a home for one or more dependents).

It also could be that, at some point, one of the head-of-household parents may seek to remarry. In such event, the live aparts have to get a formal decree of divorce before the new marriage becomes legal. Even so, the head-of-household status of the unremarried parent remains intact.

Another Status: Form 1040EZ

The five filing status checkboxes that we listed earlier appear directly on Forms 1040 and 1040A. With the growing demand for easy-to-prepare tax returns, Form 1040EZ has emerged [the "EZ" is for E-A-S-Y]. Form 1040EZ is a "no dependents" tax return. It can be used either by single filers or joint filers (married filing jointly, that is). Its full official title is: *Income Tax Return for Single and Joint Filers With No Dependents*. The includible income sources are limited strictly to wages, salaries, tips, and unemployment compensation. Any taxable interest income is limited to $400. If there are any other sources of reportable income, Form 1040EZ cannot be used.

The filing status choices on Form 1040EZ are unique. There are just two checkboxes: "Yes" or "No." An instructional side note says—

You must check Yes or No.

Before actually checking a box, the filer is asked:

Can your parents (or someone else) claim you [as a dependent] *on their return?*

Yes. Enter amount   *No. If single, enter $_____*
      from worksheet   *If married, enter $_____*
    ☐ *on back*   ☐ *See back for explanation.*

The "worksheet on back" consists of ten separate instructions. It is instruction "F" that is pertinent at this time. It reads—

Exemption amount
- *If single, enter 0*
- *If married and . . .*
  — *both you and your spouse can be claimed as dependents, enter 0*
  — *only one of you can be claimed as a dependent, enter $_____* [the allowable exemption amount for the year of filing].

There are three aspects of Form 1040EZ that make it significant to our discussion. One aspect is that it can be used by one or more children of the parents, and by one or more grandparents of the children. That is, single filers can use Form 1040EZ without jeopardizing the dependency claims of parents (or of someone else).

The second aspect of Form 1040EZ is that, if a child becomes newly married, that child *and* his or her spouse can continue to be claimed on the parent's return. More likely, though, each parent of the newly marrieds would claim his/her respective child on that parent's return. It often takes a year or two (or so) before first-time young marrieds are adequately self-supporting. The simplicity of Form 1040EZ is its most desirable characteristic. See Figure 1.5.

There is a third attractive aspect of Form 1040EZ. The grandparents do not have to be widowed to be claimed as a dependent or dependents on someone else's return. Married grandparents can be claimed as dependents, either together or separately on their children's returns. Much depends on the ability of each child to financially support his/her own parent(s). Most likely, the child of one set of grandparents would claim that grandparent (or those grandparents), while the spouse, child of another set of grandparents, would claim those grandparents. The only "catch" is that if either of the married grandparents receives any pension, annuity, or Social Security benefits, Form 1040EZ cannot be used. Instead, Form 1040A would have to be used. Even so, Form 1040A does not alter the dependency-claiming options for supporters of grandparents, whether married or widowed.

	SINGLE AND JOINT FILERS WITH NO DEPENDENTS
	Name(s), Address, Tax ID(s)
Income	1. Wages, salaries, and tips ⎯⎯⎯⎯⎯⎯ ⎯⎯⎯⎯⎯⎯⎯ 2. Interest income: $400 or less ⎯⎯⎯⎯⎯ ⎯⎯⎯⎯⎯⎯⎯ 3. Unemployment compensation ⎯⎯⎯⎯ ⎯⎯⎯⎯⎯⎯⎯ **Gross Income ▶** ⎯⎯⎯⎯⎯⎯⎯
Status	Can your parent(s) (or someone else) claim you [and your spouse, if any] on their returns? <u>Yes</u> □ *See text or official form.* (✱) <u>No</u> □ *See text or official form.*
Payments	• Payer withholdings ⎯⎯⎯⎯⎯⎯⎯⎯ ⎯⎯⎯⎯⎯⎯⎯ • Earned income credit ⎯⎯⎯⎯⎯⎯⎯ ⎯⎯⎯⎯⎯⎯⎯ **Total Payments ▶** ⎯⎯⎯⎯⎯⎯⎯
	Tax ⎯⎯⎯⎯ ; **Refund** ⎯⎯⎯⎯ ; **Amount Due** ⎯⎯⎯⎯
	(✱) If married: If 1 or both spouses as dependents; check "Yes". If **both** spouses are **not** dependents; check "No".

Fig. 1.5 - The Simplifications (and Limitations) of Form 1040EZ

When Form 1040 Required

There are two particular situations where Forms 1040A and 1040EZ cannot be used by a dependent. The situations are self-employment and capital gains. There are no suitable entries on the "short" forms for self-employment and capital gain/loss income. Only Form 1040 can be used to report said income and compute the tax thereon.

The term "self employment" applies to a dependent (or to either parent) who is worker classed as a *nonemployee*. An employee has social security and medicare automatically taken out of his compensation check(s). A nonemployee has no such withholdings taken. Consequently, a nonemployee has to file the appropriate tax schedules to assure that he or she pays the applicable social security and medicare tax. Age is NOT a factor in whether the social security/medicare tax is payable. A 10-year-old child working at "odd jobs" (such as baby sitting, trash pickup, photo shots, acting, etc.) is just as liable for such tax as is a 90-year-old grandparent earning "pin money" (such as embroidering, telling stories to children, being a companion to invalids, etc.).

The social security/medicare tax is a **flat** 15.3% of the net earnings from self employment. It applies to all net earnings of $400 or more, per year. Technically, the social security/medicare tax is called: *Self-Employment Tax.* It is computed on **Schedule SE**, which attaches to Form 1040.

Before Schedule SE can be prepared, **Schedule C**: *Profit or Loss from Business* (self employment) must be completed. It is the *net* earnings from Schedule C that go onto Schedule SE. Schedule C also attaches to Form 1040.

Capital gain or loss results when "capital assets" (stocks, bonds, contracts, real estate, tangible property items, ownership interest in a business, etc.) are sold or exchanged. The tax accounting for these transactions appears on Schedule D (Form 1040): *Capital Gains and Losses.* For each given year, the gains and losses are netted. After the netting, either a net capital gain or a net capital loss results. Any net capital loss is usable up to $3,000 for the current year. Any excess loss is carried over to the subsequent year (or years). Any net capital gain is taxed on a special schedule known as: Part IV of Schedule D.

Part IV of Schedule D is titled: *Tax Computation Using Maximum Capital Gains Rates.* Whereas ordinary tax rates extend from 10% to 38%, capital gains rates extend from 8% to 28%. Clearly, because the capital gains rates are lower, they are preferential. In the taxable income range up to $25,000 (single), both the 10% and 8% rates apply. Therefore, for family tax strategizing, if a dependent can generate capital gain instead of ordinary income, the 8% rate would apply.

2

DEPENDENTS & EXEMPTIONS

A "Dependent" Is An Individual For Whom You Provide MORE THAN HALF Of His/Her Total Support. Other Qualifications Are U.S. Citizenship (Or U.S. Residency), Some Family Relationship, And Nil Or Meager Income Of Dependent's Own. For Children, Their Progressive "Age Level" Is An Important Factor In The Type And Extent Of Support. For Each Dependent, The Primary Filer (Family Head) Gets A Tax Deduction Called: EXEMPTION AMOUNT (Adjusted Yearly For Inflation). Although A Dependent Filer Can Claim An Exemption For Himself, Strategically It Is NOT Beneficial That He Do So. The Family Head Will Lose The Exemption.

The principal characteristic of any family is having dependents. The first persons ordinarily thought of as dependents are children. That is, the natural children of the filers, their stepchildren, adopted children, grandchildren, foster children . . . and the like. A "child" is normally thought of as a young person who is not self-supporting until he/she reaches legal age. The yardstick for dependency, however, is not legal age but is the necessity for financial support.

Other persons who can qualify as dependents are parents of the filers (grandparents of the children), stepparents, parents-in-law, uncles and aunts, brothers and sisters, other relatives, and other persons who are not necessarily blood-related. As you'll see below, the IRS definition of a dependent covers a wide range of persons who financially depend upon Form 1040 filers for their housing, well-being, and support.

To tax qualify as a dependent, several "tests" must be met. These are tests of (1) relationship, (2) joint return, (3) citizenship, (4) income, and (5) support. We'll expand on these items as each becomes progressively relevant to our discussion. Needless to say, the *support* test is where most of the tax challenges arise.

For every qualified dependent, the filer is allowed a *personal exemption* amount. For 2002, the exemption amount was $3,000. Clearly, a dependent is worth tax money to the family head; order of $840 in a 28% tax bracket. At the highest individual tax bracket of about 38%, a dependent is worth $1,140 in tax dollars.

In this chapter, therefore, we want to review the qualifying ramifications of dependency status, indicate how dependents are properly claimed on Form 1040, the role of multiple support agreements, and the "comparative worth" of the exemption amount between claimant and dependent. In our discussion, we will touch rather briefly on children of divorce. This is a highly emotional issue between the two parents involved. The tax problems can be worked out only if the parents comprehend the requirements of support and housing for the children they love.

How "Dependent" is Defined

The Internal Revenue Code defines dependents in a very broad way. In doing so, it uses the term "taxpayer" as being the claimant of the dependent(s). For us, the term "taxpayer" applies to one parent or both, who are the primary filers of the family return.

More specifically, Section 152(a): *General Definition*, says—

The term "dependent" means any of the following individuals over half of whose support, for the calendar year . . ., was received from the taxpayer (or is treated . . . as received from the taxpayer):

(1)   A son or daughter of the taxpayer, or a descendant of either;

(2)   A stepson or stepdaughter of the taxpayer;

(3)   A brother, sister, stepbrother, or stepsister of the taxpayer;

(4)   The father or mother of the taxpayer, or an ancestor of either;

(5)   A stepfather or stepmother of the taxpayer;

(6)   A son or daughter of a brother or sister of the taxpayer;

(7)   A brother or sister of the father or mother of the taxpayer; [or]

(8)   A son-in-law, daughter-in-law, father-in-law, mother-in-law, brother-in-law, or sister-in-law of the taxpayer.

This tax code definition pretty well exhausts the **relationship test** of a qualified dependent. The common theme is some vestige of a blood relationship derived from a legal marriage. Of significance to note is that a relationship once established by marriage *does not end* upon divorce or death. Although the blood relationship may not end with divorce or death, financial dependence itself may well end.

Subsection 152(a)(9) addresses a "member of the household" who is not a blood relative. The wording for this dependency provision is not brilliantly clear, but you can get the point. It says—

An individual (other than . . . the spouse . . . of the taxpayer) who, for the [full] *taxable year of the taxpayer, has as his principal place of abode the home of the taxpayer and is a member of the taxpayer's household.*

This provision is directed primarily at foster children (placed temporarily), unemployed adults (in temporary need), and unmarried "live-ins." Any expense-sharing arrangement of mutual benefit to the homeowner and the household member is treated as NOT a "dependency" situation. Similarly, for a nanny performing housekeeping services for working parents of minor children.

Other Definitional Aspects

Section 152(a) clearly sets forth a support test before any of the persons listed can be claimed as a dependent. The test is: *over half of whose support* is furnished by the taxpayer claimant. There are regulatory requirements as to what constitutes "support." We'll present these requirements below. Above all else, support is the key test for dependency qualification.

Section 152(b)(3) addresses the citizenship status of a dependent. This subsection says, in part—

*The term "dependent" does not include an individual who is not a citizen or national of the U.S. **unless** such individual is a **resident** of the U.S. or of a country contiguous to the U.S.* [Emphasis added.]

The "residency test" is intended to exclude brothers, sisters, parents, cousins, and other relatives of U.S. naturalized citizens who live in a foreign country other than Canada and Mexico.

There is also a "joint return" test. It is not succinctly defined by law or regulation; it is defined more by administrative practice. The general rule is that a claimed dependent may not file a joint return, except to claim a refund. A husband cannot claim his wife as a dependent . . . nor vice versa. They do not need to; each is a primary filer of his/her own. On a joint return, the separate dependents of either spouse may be included. So-called "common law" marriages are not recognized for joint return purposes.

Age "Levels" of Children

A "child" is tax defined as a son, stepson, daughter, or stepdaughter of the taxpayer. It makes no difference whether a child is natural or adopted. The term also extends to one who—

(i) has not attained the age of 19 at the close of the calendar year in which the taxable year of the taxpayer begins, or
(ii) is a student who has not attained the age of 24 at the close of such calendar year [IRC Sec. 151(c)(1)(B)].

Thus, all parents face an age span of from birth to 24 years for which a child may be claimed as their dependent. This dependency persists irrespective of the child's income, if any.

Throughout this 24-year age span, there are six tax-distinct age levels of dependent children. Focusing on "age level," rather than on a specific age, markedly helps in strategizing the family finances and tax benefits.

First, there is an *age 13 level.* This is the age at which, traditionally, children emerge from being "minors" to spring into being "teenagers." While under age 13, the parents may claim a very worthwhile dependent care credit against their income tax. Under age 13 is also the level for which baby sitting and nanny care services are required. If such services are performed in the household, there is likelihood that a "Nanny Tax" will have to be paid. Said tax is a real pain. Many single- and two-working parents will agonize long and hard over it.

Second, there is an *age 14 level.* This is the threshold below which parents may elect to pay the child's tax on the child's investment income (interest, dividends, capital gain) up to $7,000. This is also the age at which a child may start earning tax accountable money and having to file his/her own income tax return.

Third, there is an *age 17 level.* This is the age up to which special "child credits" apply to middle-income parents, and to which "earned income" credits apply to lower-income parents. This is also the age level where high school "drop out" occurs, and the children veer from parental guidance. Often, substantial additional financial support is required, for which there are few, if any, tax benefits to the parents.

Fourth, there is an *age 19 level.* By this age, most children are out of high school, out of trade school, or out of farm school. If not headed for college, they enter the workforce or the military. This is the age at which many parents start losing their child as a dependent, particularly if the child earns $7,000 or more.

Fifth, there is an *age 21* level. In the federal domain, this is the age of young adulthood. It is also the age where, if any "gifts to minors" trusts have been set up (by grandparents or by others), the accumulations of property and income to that point pass legally to the donee child [Section 2503(c)(2)(A)]. This can become the first test of whether your child is a spendthrift.

And, sixth, there is the *age 24 level.* This is the age of college or graduate school where a child can still be claimed as a dependent, even though he/she is not living at home most of the year. The requirement is that the "student" attend a recognized educational organization not less than five calendar months of the year [IRC Section 151(c)(4)]. As long as the child is attending school in good faith, certain "educational credits" and "student loan interest" deductions may accrue to the parents' benefit. We'll cover these and other related educational activities in Chapters 6 and 7.

What Constitutes "Support"?

Other than a claimant's own children, the age of a dependent is not an issue. Whether a dependent is 30, 50, 70 years or older, it makes no difference. What makes a difference is the amount of total income from all sources (public, private, and nontaxable) that the dependent receives. If that income is at or below the national poverty level, the validity of a dependency claim is rarely ever challenged. As a rough guideline, the "poverty level" in the U.S. is about $120 per **week**, or about $6,000 per year (per adult person).

A dependent is not required to live in poverty. It is just that any support provided that is above the poverty level has to be justified with adequate documentation. With poverty in mind, therefore, what constitutes "support" for dependency-claiming purposes?

The answer is found in IRS Regulation 1.152-1(a)(2)(i): *General definition of support.* This regulation reads essentially in full as—

> *For purposes of determining whether or not an individual received, for a given calendar year, over half of his support from the taxpayer, there shall be taken into account the amount of support received from the taxpayer as compared to the entire amount of support which the individual received from all sources, including support which the individual himself supplied. The term "support" includes food, shelter, clothing, medical and dental care, education, and the like. Generally, the amount of an item of support will be the amount of expense incurred by the one furnishing such item.* [Emphasis added.]

The idea behind the above regulation is that all money actually spent for the support of a dependent counts. There is no standard amount. Therefore, the first task is to record on a monthly basis how much was actually spent. Disregard (for the time being) who contributed the money. What did it cost to support (nonlavishly) the lifestyle of the dependent, taking into account his age, aspirations, physical impairments, health needs, and talents. Included in such determination are amounts spent for transportation, entertainment, hygiene, and communication (phone, cell, fax, e-mail, Internet access). This is "Step 1" in the support process.

The term "shelter" used in the regulation above includes all forms of housing, whether temporary or permanent. It is the *rent equivalent* of mortgage payments, property tax, and hazard insurance. Additionally, there are repairs, maintenance, security, and utilities to be factored in. Where shelter is shared by all members of a household, its total cost is prorated among all members. For example, if the rent equivalent of a family home is $1,500 per month, and there are five persons living in that home, the "per individual" shelter cost would be $300 [$1,500 ÷ 5 persons]. Similarly, for food, maintenance, and utilities. This is "Step 2" in the support process.

The next support activity ("Step 3") is to establish the amount that each contributor pays, including the dependent. In the case of children, the parent or parents are generally the primary contributors (as they should be). Any support contribution by a child is usually minimal. A child is not required to use his part-time earnings or savings to support himself. In contrast, an adult dependent is expected to use his current earnings, pensions, social security benefits, and IRA distributions for his own support. Where there is any form of public assistance or insurance proceeds, these are treated as "money spent" on support of the individual intended.

And, finally, "Step 4" is to determine, among multiple contributors, who contributed more than 50% (*over half*) of the individual's total support. Once each support contributor is identified in terms of specific dollars per month, it is relatively easy to conclude who is the primary contributor.

Because of the importance of the above, we tie all four steps together for you in Figure 2.1. As this figure implies, when a claimant is challenged (by the IRS or by some supporter), a lot of "pencil work" has to be done. This means keeping good records when the 50% support mark is touch and go.

BASIC PREMISE	Every dependent requires for support separate expenditures for - • Food • Clothing • Shelter • Medical • Communication • Education • Recreation • Hygiene • Transportation • Etc.
Step 1	Determine cost of those items furnished individually to each dependent; categorize and tally.
Step 2	Prorate those costs that are shared mutually by all dependents (housing, insurance, utilities, etc.); categorize and tally.
TOTALIZE	Tally TOTAL SUPPORT COST for each dependent (regardless of source).
Step 3	Establish amount that each contributor pays for each dependent. Include that paid by yourself, dependent, relatives, insurance, nontaxable sources, and public assistance.
Step 4	Establish your % of total support for each dependent. Divide your payment by the sum-total of all contributions. If your % is more than 50%, that dependent qualifies on your return.
CAUTION	Keep copious worksheet notes, in event of challenge by IRS or by some contributor.

Fig. 2.1 - Steps for Determining "Over 50%" of Dependent's Support

Multiple Support Agreements

Where there is an adult dependent, such as a parent of the claimant or other dear relative, support is often furnished by multiple persons. For example, consider a dependent who is elderly, invalid, and a victim of Alzheimer's disease. The total cost of supporting such an individual is beyond the financial capability of the claimant caretaker. Such support can be particularly burdensome where other dependents, such as children, are involved. Consequently, brothers and sisters of the claimant and other close family members are imposed upon to contribute. The common result is that no one taxpayer can show that he contributed more than 50% of that dependent's total support. What happens in this case? Fortunately, there is a sensible way to handle the situation.

Section 152(c): *Multiple Support Agreements*, specifically addresses such concern. Its key wording is—

Over half of the support of an individual for a calendar year shall be treated as received from the taxpayer if—

(1) **no one person** *contributed over half of such support;*

(2) *over half of such support was received from persons each of whom, but for the fact that he did not contribute over half of such support, would have been entitled to claim such an individual as a dependent . . .;*

(3) *the taxpayer contributed* **over 10 percent** *of such support; and*

(4) *each person described in paragraph (2) (other than the taxpayer) who contributed over 10 percent of such support files a* **written declaration** *. . . that he will not claim such individual as a dependent . . . in such calendar year.* [Emphasis added.]

The reference to a "written declaration" means the express use of IRS Form 2120: *Multiple Support Declaration.* Each person (other than the agreed-upon claimant) contributing more than 10% to a named dependent's support prepares Form 2120 on his own. This form is prepared *each year* that an agreement is in effect. Each preparer of Form 2120 affixes his signature, name, address, and social security number to the statement that:

I agree not to claim this person as a dependent on my Federal income tax return for taxable year _____.

There may be, and often are, multiple such forms. As depicted in Figure 2.2, the claimant collects the Forms 2120 from all disclaimants, and attaches the bundle to his own Form 1040 for the taxable year at issue.

Children of Divorced Parents

When the parents of one or more children are divorced or separated, which parent gets to claim the children as dependents? This is a nationwide emotional issue of longstanding. To neutralize the endless bickering and court hearings that take place, many states

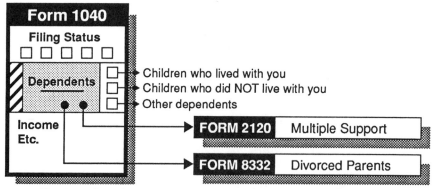

Fig. 2.2 - Attachment of "Support Declarations" re Dependents

are leaning towards *joint custody* assignments. Technically and legally each parent is responsible for each child's total support. Under such arrangement, neither spouse can show that he or she provided over half of a child's support for the calendar year. What happens in this case?

Be introduced now to IR Code Section 152(e): *Support Test in Case of Child of Divorced Parents.* The essence of this section is that—

> *If a child . . . receives over half of his support . . . from his parents—*
> (i)   *who are divorced or legally separated . . ., or*
> (ii) *who are separated under a written agreement, or*
> (iii) *who live apart at all times during the last 6 months of the calendar year, and*
> (iv) *such child is in the custody of one or both parents for more than one-half of the calendar year*
> [then] *such child **shall be treated** . . . as receiving over half of his support . . . from the parent having custody for a greater portion of the calendar year.*

This is known as the custodial parent "presumption" rule [Sec. 152(e)(**1**)]. This rule greatly simplifies the pencil-work necessary in Figure 2.1. The rule requires that at least one parent keep a record of the number of nights a child spent in his or her household throughout the year. The parent that can show the greater number of overnight stays for the year gets to claim that child as a dependent. That parent becomes the tax recognized *custodial parent*.

There **is**, however, an exception to the custodial parent rule. The exception is Section 152(e)(2): *Exception Where Custodial Parent Releases Claim*. This noncustodial rule says that—

> *If the custodial parent signs a **written declaration** . . . that* [he or she] *will not claim such child as a dependent for any* [designated year or years], *and the noncustodial parent attaches such written declaration to* [his or her] *tax return for the taxable year . . . the child **shall be treated** as having received over half of his support . . . from the noncustodial parent.* [Emphasis added.]

The reference to a "written declaration" means the use of Form 8332: *Release of Claim to Exemption for Child of Divorced or Separated Parents*. Note that this form uses the word "exemption" — rather than "dependent" — in its official title. An *exemption* claim is the same as a *dependency* claim. We'll explain this point shortly.

Meanwhile, Form 8332 consists of two parts, namely:

Part I   Release of Claim to Exemption for Current Year
Part II Release of Claim to Exemption for Future Years

Each part is signaturized by the custodial parent who is releasing the claim to the noncustodial parent. The statement being addressed is:

> *I agree not to claim an exemption for* (name(s) of child or children) *for the tax year(s)* _____ .

The name (and social security number) of the noncustodial parent who is being allowed to claim the dependent child or children is entered at the top of Form 8332. The social security number of each affected child should also be entered. A preprinted instruction on Form 8332 says—

> *ATTACH to noncustodial parent's return EACH YEAR exemption is claimed.*

Form 8332 attaches as shown in Figure 2.2.

Why would a custodial parent give up his/her child dependency exemption claim?

It is a matter of tax benefit trade-offs. If the custodial parent receives child support payments, such amounts are NOT tax reportable income. That is, child support payments are not taxable to the recipient (payee) parent, nor are they tax deductible to the payer (noncustodial) parent. To partly compensate for this inequity, the payer parent gets a dependency exemption. A dependency exemption is a separate deduction of its own. This is the kind of thing that reasonable parents — even though divorced or separated — can strategize for their mutual tax benefit.

Dependency Exemption: How Much?

Section 151 of the IR Code is titled: *Allowance of Deductions for Personal Exemptions.* This wording alone tells you that there is a tax deduction for each personal exemption amount. Confirmation of this fact is in subsection 151(a) which reads—

> *In the case of an individual, the exemptions provided by this section **shall be allowed** as deductions in computing taxable income.* [Emphasis added.]

Here you have it! A "personal exemption" is a deductible amount that you use when computing your taxable income on Form 1040. Thus, said exemption is a valuable tax-saving device.

What the above title does not convey is that there are **two** types of personal exemptions. There is a *filer exemption,* and there is a *dependency exemption.* In the case of a joint return, there are two filer exemptions: one for "yourself" and one for "spouse." Confirmation of these two types of exemptions can be found in subsection 151(b): *Taxpayer and Spouse, and in subsection 151(c): Additional Exemption for Dependents.* All individual exemption amounts are the same.

In 1988, Congress set the exemption amount at $2,000 per individual [Sec. 151(d)(1)]. In 1990, Congress added subsection 151(d)(4) to adjust the exemption amount for cost-of-living inflation. For 2002, the inflation adjusted exemption amount was $3,000. This figure will increase in forthcoming years.

At $3,000 of exemption deduction per dependent, what is a filer's savings in actual tax dollars (rounded)?

The savings amount depends, of course, on the tax rate bracket of the filer (you). For the 2002 tax rate brackets (rounded), the savings were as follows:

Tax Bracket	Tax Savings
10%	$ 300
15 %	$ 450
25%	$ 750
30%	$ 900
35 %	$1,050
38%	$1,140

If you and your spouse had a taxable income in the range of $100,000 to $150,000, your tax bracket would be about 30%. If you had four dependents, your tax savings would be $3,600. If you had six dependents, your savings would be $5,400. This kind of tax savings is no small piece of family change.

How Exemptions Are Claimed

If you have one or more dependents who are "tax qualified" (as previously described), you list each one on Page 1 of Form 1040. The specific entry point is at line **6c:** *Dependents*. This line is conspicuously displayed in the horizontally ruled-off portion of Form 1040, side labeled: *Exemptions*. In an edited arrangement, we present this portion of Form 1040 in Figure 2.3.

When reviewing Figure 2.3, we suggest you do so in three steps. Step 1 is the filer checkboxes; Step 2 is the dependency listing; and Step 3 is the counting of each type of exemption claimed. Steps 1 and 3 are self-explanatory in Figure 2.3.

As to Step 2, you are required to state each dependent's full name [Col. (1)], social security number [Col. (2)], and his/her relationship to you [Col. (3)]. On this matter, Section 151(e) titled: *Identifying Information Required*, reads—

Form 1040	IDENTIFICATION BLOCK	Your SSN
		Spouse's SSN

Exemptions	Primary filer			Exemption Counter
	☐ Spouse ☐ Yourself			
If more than 6 dependents attach "continuation sheet".	**Dependents**			☐
	(1) Name	(2) SSN	(3) Relation	☐
				☐
				☐
				☐
	Continue as needed			
	Total number of exemptions claimed ▶			☐

See official form

Fig. 2.3 - Claiming Dependency Exemptions on Form 1040 (Primary Filer)

No exemption shall be allowed under this section with respect to any individual unless the SSN [Social Security Number] of such individual is included on the return claiming the exemption.

Instructions to Form 1040 for Line 6c, Column (2) say—

You must enter each dependent's social security number (SSN). If you do not enter the correct SSN at the time we process your return, we may disallow the exemption claimed for that dependent and reduce or disallow any other tax benefits . . . based on the dependent. . . . To apply for an SSN, get Form SS-5 from your local Social Security Administration (SSA) office or call the SSA at 1-800-772-1213. Fill in Form SS-5 and return it to the SSA [not to the IRS].

If a dependent child is born during the year, you get the full exemption allowance for that year. If a child is born and dies before the calendar year ends, attach a copy of the child's birth certificate and enter "DIED" in column (2). If some other dependent dies during the year, you also get the full exemption allowance. However, enter "DECEASED on ____(date)____" as a footnote to column (3): *Relationship to you.*

When a Dependent Files

Generally speaking, when a dependent earns more than his personal exemption amount ($3,000 in 2002), he is required to file a tax return. Even when he does, he may pay no income tax. This is particularly so if his earnings in excess of the exemption amount are equal to or less than the standard deduction amount ($4,700 in 2002) for a single filer. The strategizing challenge, therefore, is to find that "break point" below or above which it is more tax beneficial to the primary filer (family head) to claim the exemption amount, rather than sacrificing it to the dependent filer.

To bring the break point challenge into perspective, we present in Figure 2.4 the basic factors involved. Note that the tax accounting sequence is:

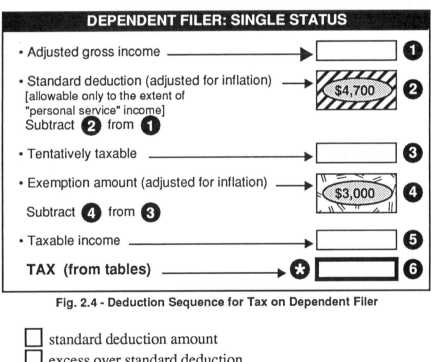

Fig. 2.4 - Deduction Sequence for Tax on Dependent Filer

☐ standard deduction amount
☐ excess over standard deduction
☐ personal exemption amount
☐ excess over personal exemption

Whereas the standard deduction amount differs for each filing status, the personal exemption amount is fixed (except for inflation adjustments).

To illustrate the breakpoint effort required, let us assume that a dependent earned an income of $5,000; $6,000; $7,000; $8,000; and $9,000. He is a single filer, and thus would be in the 10% or 15% tax bracket. After the standard deduction, the tax dollar differences between the dependent foregoing the exemption amount and claiming it, are as follows:

	Tax without exemption	Tax with exemption	Difference (rounded)
at $5,000	40	zero	40
" 6,000	140	zero	140
" 7,000	240	zero	240
" 8,000	340	40	300
" 9,000	440	140	300

Based on these figures, the break point (for 2002) is approximately $7,700. It will be slightly higher in subsequent years.

Most primary filers, if not in a higher bracket, are generally in the 25% to 30% tax brackets (say, 28% on average). They have to be, in order to support an entourage of dependents. An exemption amount at 28% tax is worth $840 in savings. As illustrated above, isn't it better that the primary filer claim the exemption amount rather than the dependent filer?

This exemption benefit to the primary filer is the very reason that Forms 1040EZ, 1040A, and 1040 carry a precautionary note at the "yourself" checkbox. The preprinted precaution reads—

> *If your parent (or someone else) can claim you as a dependent on his or her* [or their] *tax return,* **do not** *check box 6a* [yourself].

This is the premise that we tried to stress in Chapter 1. Only one claimant is entitled to use the allowable exemption amount.

3

DEPENDENT CARE CREDIT

If You Have Minor Children Or Disabled Adults To Support While Being Gainfully Employed, A Dependent Care CREDIT Or A Dependent Care EXCLUSION Is Allowable. To Claim The Credit/Exclusion, Form 2441 Must Be Used. This Requires Identification Of Each "Care Provider" And The Amount Paid. Qualifying Expenses Are Those For HOUSEHOLD SERVICES (Cleaning, Babysitting, Food, Safety, Etc.) Which Are Necessary For The Well-Being Of "Qualified Persons." Whichever Benefit Is Sought, The Maximum Allowable Is A $960 Credit Or A $5,000 Exclusion. A Lesser Amount May Apply Under "Smallest Of" Rule.

With the rise of two-career marriages and single-parent homes, there has grown the need for household care of dependents while the breadwinner is working or seeking work. This is especially true where the dependents are minor children or disabled adults. The reality is that necessary expenditures are made within the household in order to earn money outside of the household. The money so earned is income taxed.

In a business situation, the expenses incurred in earning taxable money are tax deductible . . . to the extent that they are ordinary and necessary. In a family situation, there is no comparable deduction for expenses incurred for earning income. Instead, a credit/exclusion for child- and dependent-care expenses is available. The allowability of this credit-exclusion is a function of the nature of household services rendered, and the amount of earnings derived by you and your spouse (if any).

A "credit/exclusion" differs markedly from the exemption deduction that we described in the latter portion of Chapter 2. Whereas a "deduction" is applied for arriving at taxable income, a "credit" is applied after the tax is determined. An "exclusion" is an amount not reported as earned income. The result is that your tax is reduced "off the top." You have a choice of claiming either a credit or an exclusion, or a combination of the two, so long as a prescribed maximum computational base is not exceeded.

The amount of dependent care credit/exclusion is computed on Form 2441: *Child and Dependent Care Expenses.* As of 2003, this form uses a credit computational base of not more than $3,000 for one qualifying dependent, or not more than $6,000 for two or more such persons. The exclusion computational base is $5,000 ($2,500 if married filing separately). The "not more than" means that if the lower of two spousal incomes is less than the applicable computational base, the lower earnings become the computational base. This often means less credit or exclusion.

While widely used, Form 2441 is not as self-explanatory as one would like. Consequently, we will devote the principal portion of this chapter to this one form and its statutory background. We have a lot of pointers and precautions to tell you about when using Form 2441. If you have young children (under age 13), handicapped dependents (regardless of age), or elderly persons in your household, the dependent care credit/exclusion is well worthwhile.

Basic Law: Section 21

Section 21 of the Internal Revenue Code addresses the allowability of a *credit*: **not** that of an exclusion. The section is long-titled: *Expenses for Household and Dependent Care Services Necessary for Gainful Employment.* This wording alone gives you the gist of Section 21. In a nutshell, in order to get the tax credit, the dependent care service must be "necessary for gainful employment." Here the term "employment" means self-employment as well as employee employment. If, on a joint return, one spouse is not gainfully employed, there is no credit for dependent care. You may incur the expenses but you get no tax credit when not taxably employed.

Subsection 21(a): *Allowance of credit*, generalizes the requirements this way—

> *If . . . an individual . . . maintains a household which includes as a member one or more qualifying individuals . . ., there shall be allowed as a credit against* [his] *tax . . . an amount equal to the applicable percentage of the employment-related expenses . . . paid by such individual during the taxable year.* [Emphasis added.]

For incomes over $30,000, the "applicable percentage" is 20% of the employment-related expenses not in excess of $3,000 for one individual, or $6,000 for two or more qualifying individuals. Thus, the maximum possible credit against your tax is $600 for one qualifying person, or $1,200 for two or more such persons.

Note in the citation above that the word "dependent" is not used; instead, the term "qualifying individual" is used. A qualifying individual is definitionally more specific than an ordinary dependent, and is limited to—

(A) a dependent child who is under age 13,
(B) a dependent who is physically or mentally incapable of caring for himself/herself (regardless of age), or
(C) your spouse if he/she is physically or mentally incapable of self-care.

If Married, Must File Jointly

One particular special rule that requires emphasis is Section 21(e)(2): *Married Couples Must File Joint Return*. The clarity of the "must" is stated as—

> *If the taxpayer is married at the close of the taxable year, the credit shall be allowed under subsection (a) only if the taxpayer and his spouse file a joint return for the taxable year.* [Emphasis added.]

The implication is that, if you are not "unmarried" at the end of the year, a joint return is required. There is a special "smallest of" reason for this.

Buried in Section 21(d): *Earned Income Limitation*, there is a **smallest of** rule. Such rule is not actually stated this way. The "smallest of" derives from such tax-legal phrases as—

> *(1)* *The amount of the employment-related expenses . . . which* ***may be*** *taken into account under subsection (a)* ***shall not exceed* . . .**
>
> > *(B)* *the* ***lesser of*** *such individual's earned income or the earned income of his spouse for such taxable year.* [Emphasis added.}

As a matter of fact, the "smallest of" appears distinctly on Form 2441: *Child and Dependent Care Expenses.*

In two separate places on Form 2441, the following computational chronology appears:

1. Expenses incurred. $_____
   [NOT MORE than the statutory maximum computational base.]

2. YOUR earned income   _____

3. SPOUSE'S earned income   _____

4. Enter the SMALLEST OF 1, 2, or 3   _____

If you and your spouse file separate returns, there is no way to correlate your incomes with the "smallest of" above. If you have only one qualifying dependent, you cannot split the dependent care credit. If you have two or more dependents, you can split them and each spouse claim one credit. But, to do so, you have to maintain two separate households. Consequently, unless you are legally divorced or legally separated, married filing jointly is required for the dependent care credit.

Identifications Required

Three types of persons must be identified on Form 2441. There are — as always — the name and social security number of the filer/claimant/taxpayer. This name (and Tax ID) appears at the top of the form. In the case of a joint return, the name (and Tax ID) that first appears on the front of Form 1040 is used. This is that very first line that asks for "your name" *and* "your social security number." If the spousal name and Tax IDs are switched between Forms 1040 and 2441, any claimed credit amount will be computer disallowed.

The second identification requirement is the name, *address*, and Tax ID of the care provider. A care provider can be either an individual or an entity (such as a church, school, day care center, etc.). For individuals, the SSN is used; for entities, the EIN (Employer Identification Number) is used. If the provider is a tax-exempt entity, enter "Tax-Exempt" for its ID. The identifications are entered in Part I: *Persons or Organizations Who Provided the Care — you MUST complete this part.* Form 2441 provides space for two care providers. Preprinted instructions say: *If more space is needed, use the bottom of page 2.* Also entered in Part I is the *Amount paid* to each care provider. Show the total amount actually paid *in* the calendar year, whether by you, your employer, or a combination thereof.

Separate instructions caution you to use **Form W-10**: *Dependent Care Provider's Identification and Certification*, to obtain the provider's Tax ID. The instructions also say that if you do not enter the provider's ID, your credit/exclusion claim will be disallowed

> *. . . unless you can show you used due diligence in trying to get the information required.*

Instructions on Form W-10 tell you what to do to establish "due diligence" on your part.

The third identification requirement on Form 2441 pertains to the qualifying persons whom you claim as dependents on page 1 of Form 1040. Again, the name and SSN of each such qualifying individual are required. If one of the persons is a child who turned age 13 during the year, that child is a "qualifying person" only for the part of the year he or she was under 13. A spouse is a qualifying person only if he or she is—

physically or mentally incapable of caring for himself [herself] [IRC Sec. 21(b)(1)(C)].

The qualifying-person information is entered on line 1 in Part II: *Information About Your Qualifying Person(s)*.

There are only two spaces in Part II for your qualifying persons. Instructions tell you to attach a statement for more than two persons. But why do so? You can only claim the credit for the two highest qualifying expenses paid. For example, suppose you had four qualifying persons, as follows. The maximum expenses you could claim are:

	Example *Expense amount*	*Maximum* *Qualifying amount*
Person 1	$ 3,000	$3,000
Person 2	3,500	3,000
Person 3	2,000	-0-
Person 4	2,500	-0-
	$11,000	$6,000

To put the above identifying matters in perspective, we present Figure 3.1. This figure is an abbreviation of page 1 of Form 2441. Unless the indicated spaces are filled in properly, the rest of the form is meaningless. When claiming a tax credit (or tax exclusion) you have to be far more precise than when claiming a tax deduction. A credit is a dollar-for-dollar offset against regular tax.

What Expenses Qualify?

Column (c), Part II of Form 2441 carries the heading:

Qualified expenses you incurred and paid in ___[year]___ *for the person listed in column (a).*

Form 2441	CHILD and DEPENDENT CARE EXPENSES	Year
YOUR name & SSN		As shown on Form 1040

Part I — Persons or Organizations Who Provided the Care

(a) Name	(b) Address	(c) Tax ID	(d) Amount

Instructions

Part II — Credit for Child & Dependent Care Expenses

(a) Name - first	last	(b) SSN	(c) Qualified Expense

More instructions

Part II - CREDIT Part III - EXCLUSION *See Text*	• Allowable expenses _____ • Your earned income _____ • Spouse's earned income _____ • Enter "smallest of" _____

Fig. 3.1 - Persons, Entities, & Household Expenses Identified on Form 2441

This heading raises the obvious question: What expenses qualify for the credit? The heading also emphasizes the point that the expenses must be "incurred and paid" in the calendar year for which the credit is claimed.

Section 21(b)(2): *Employment-related expenses*, points to those expenses necessary for (i) *household services*, and (ii) *care of a qualifying individual*. When combined, these are expenses incurred—

> *only . . . to enable the taxpayer* [claimant] *to be gainfully employed for any period for which there are one or more qualifying individuals.* [Emphasis added.]

The term "household services" means those needed to run the home for the qualifying person or persons. They include the services of a cook, maid, babysitter, housekeeper, or cleaning person, when performed, at least partly, for the care of the qualifying person(s). The costs for a chauffeur or gardener are *not* included as household services. Nor do the costs for services performed outside of your home qualify, such as at a camp where a minor child stays overnight. Day-care services outside of your home for children and seniors qualify, so long as the dependent returns home each night.

The term "care of a qualifying individual" includes all costs necessary for the well-being and protection of each dependent. This includes food, shelter, utilities, safety devices, instructional toys, handicap aids, etc. Clothing, entertainment, and transportation are not included, nor is the cost of schooling the moment a child enters first grade or above.

Qualified expenses are those which are actually paid from taxable sources of income. Consequently, any child support or dependent care payments received that are used for the items above do **not** count. This is because such receipts are not taxable as income. The whole idea of the dependent care credit (and other credits in subsequent chapters) is to reduce, partially, your *taxable* income. The less your taxable income, the less your tax.

Dependent Care Assistance

The very last sentence in subsection 21(c) says that the $3,000/$6,000 dollar limitation—

shall be reduced by the aggregate amount excludable from gross income under section 129 for the taxable year.

We know that you are probably asking: "What is Section 129?"

Section 129 is a special provision for dependent-care-assistance programs which are paid for, sponsored by, or provided by your employer (or by your spouse's employer). The extent of an employer's "assistance" is limited to $5,000 on a joint return. In the event of a separate return by a married individual, the employer amount is limited to $2,500. Thus, if there are two working spouses, each with the same or a different sponsoring employer, the spouses can file separate returns, and each could get up to $2,500 assistance for qualifying dependents. This separate-return feature differs markedly from the joint return requirement of Section 21.

Whereas Section 21 offers a credit benefit, Section 129 offers an *exclusion* benefit. A "credit" is the reduction of tax after applying the filing status rates to taxable income. An "exclusion," on the other hand, is the authorized *omission* from gross income of the employee being employer assisted. One's "gross income" is that amount entered in box 1 of Form W-2: *Wage and Tax Statement.* The "box 1" is labeled: *Wages, tips, other compensation.*

The functional distinction between an exclusion and a credit is portrayed in Figure 3.2. As so indicated, an exclusion benefits the commencement of a return. In contrast, the benefit of a credit comes when a return is nearly complete. Generally, an exclusion is more beneficial for higher income filers.

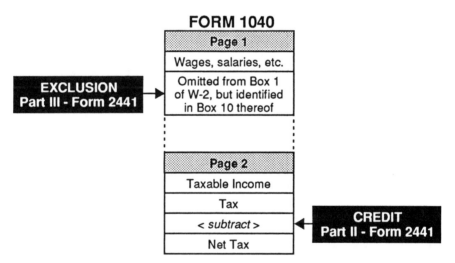

Fig. 3.2 - Distinction Between Tax "Exclusion" and Tax "Credit"

The exclusion aspects of Figure 3.2 are authorized by Section 129(a)(1): *Exclusion; In General.* This section reads essentially in full as—

> *Gross income of an employee does not include amounts paid or incurred by the employer for dependent care assistance provided to such employee if the assistance is furnished pursuant to a [qualified] program.*

Subsection 129(d) defines a qualified dependent-care-assistance program in about 500 tax-legal words. Needless to say, only well established companies can afford to sponsor such programs. Those employers who do offer a program are required to indicate in box 10 of Form W-2 the dollar amount of assistance provided. The "box 10" is labeled: *Dependent care benefits.* If an employer provides more than the $2,500/$5,000 limitation amounts, the excess assistance amount is included in box 1 (gross wages) of the assisted employee. This way, the employer gets a business expense deduction for all dependent-care assistance provided.

Exclusion on Part III, Form 2441

Form 2441 is arranged into three parts. They are—

Part I: Persons or Organizations Who Provide the Care
Part II: Credit for Child and Dependent Care Expenses
Part III: Dependent Care Benefits (allowable as an exclusion)

At the end of Part I, there is a boxed-in-bold question which asks:

You signify your "Yes" or "No" answer by hand-circling (with pen or pencil) the corresponding words. If you answer "Yes," enter in Part I your employer's name in column (**a**); enter "See W-2" in column (**b**); leave columns (**c**) and (**d**) blank. Recall Figure 3.1.

Part III is where the computational action lies with respect to those assistance benefits provided by your employer. This is a 10-step computation which we abbreviate in Figure 3.3. The general idea is to establish your **allowable excluded benefits** by the "smallest of" routine mentioned previously.

If it turns out that your allowable exclusion amount is *less than* that amount shown in box 10 of your W-2, the excess becomes a taxable benefit. For example, suppose box 10 shows an assistance amount of $5,000. At Step 9 in Figure 3.3, suppose the allowable exclusion is $4,000. Thus, the taxable portion of the $5,000 benefit

Part III	DEPENDENT CARE BENEFITS		Form 2441
1	Enter amount of dependent care benefits shown **in Box 10** of your Form(s) W-2	1	
2	Enter amount forfeited, if any	2	< >
3	Subtract Step 2 from Step 1	3	
4	Enter total of **qualified expenses** paid in current year	4	
5	Enter **smaller of** Step 3 or Step 4	5	
6	Enter **your** earned income	6	
7	Enter **spouse's** earned income (if married filing separately, see instructions)	7	
8	Enter **smallest of** Steps 5, 6, or 7	8	
9	**Excluded benefits.** Enter the **smaller of** • Step 8, or • $5,000 ($2,500 if married filing separately)	9	
10	**Taxable benefits.** Subtract Step 9 from Step 3. If zero or less, enter zero. Otherwise, enter amount on *Wages, salaries* line on Form 1040 with the notation "DCB".	10	

Continuation stops when Step 9 is less than $5,000 / $2,500

Fig. 3.3 - Steps for Ascertaining Allowable Exclusion Benefits

is $1,000 ($5,000 – 4,000). This $1,000 would show up at Step 10 in Figure 3.3. Instructions preprinted at Step 10 tell you to include the $2,000 in *Wages, salaries, tips, etc.* as income on page 1 of your Form 1040. You indicate the amount included with the letters "DCB" followed by the dollar amount. You make a hand entry to this effect on the dotted line which follows the words: *Wages, salaries, etc.*

In other words, the employer amount entered in box 10 of your W-2 is not, necessarily, all excludable from your gross wages. Your employer was allowed to treat it as such because he does not know, nor does he need to know, what your "smallest of" computation will be.

Should your excluded benefits in Part III be less than the maximum credit benefits in Part II, you are still allowed to claim any remaining credit amount. Instructions preprinted below Part III tell you how to do this. You cannot get both the maximum exclusion amount *and* the maximum credit amount. But you can get part of each. To do so, your allowable exclusion amount is first subtracted from the credit limitation amount. Then you use Part II to compute the remaining credit allowable.

For example, suppose your excluded amount was $4,000 for two or more dependents. Subtracting $4,000 from the $6,000 credit limitation amount would permit you to claim a credit based on $2,000 ($6,000 – 4,000). If you otherwise qualified, the actual credit against your tax would be $400 ($2,000 x 20%). This is an example where you could have a "part-exclusion" of $4,000 and a "part-credit" of $400.

Exclusion or Credit: Which is Better?

In the simplified example above, the exclusion amount was $4,000. At a 28% taxable income bracket (for joint filers), the "tax worth" of a $4,000 exclusion would be $1,120 ($4,000 x 28%). If, instead of being an exclusion amount, the $4,000 were a credit computation base, its tax worth would be $800 ($4,000 x 20%). Here, the 20% is an "applicable credit percentage." Be aware that this 20% has no direct correlation with one's taxable income bracket. On this (rather oversimplified) analysis alone, the exclusion tax benefits are clearly more preferential than the credit tax benefits.

As a rough rule of thumb, we can say quite categorically that, if your gross wages (for yourself and spouse) exceed $100,000, the exclusion route is the better way to go. That is, provided your employer, or your spouse's employer, offers some program of dependent-care assistance [Section 129(d)].

If your gross wages (including those of your spouse) are between $50,000 and $100,000, the credit route may be the better way to go. This is because you might likely be in the 15% taxable income bracket (especially if you had a lot of itemized personal deductions). At such tax rate, the $5,000 maximum exclusion would be tax worth $750. If, instead, you chose the credit route, your tax worth of $5,000 would be $1,000 ($5,000 x 20%). However, keep in mind that the maximum credit base for two or more qualifying persons is $6,000.

Here's another way of stating the above. If you are in the 28% or higher taxable income bracket, the exclusion benefits are definitely more advantageous. But, if you are in the 15% taxable income bracket, the credit route is the better way to go. In this lower tax bracket, even if your employer offers you a dependent-care assistance package, it is not mandatory that you participate in it. Forego the assistance and use Part II of Form 2441, exclusively.

There is still another point favoring the exclusion route. The $5,000 exclusion limit is **not** predicated upon having two or more qualifying dependents. Having only one dependent — who requires care while you are gainfully employed — can qualify you for the $5,000 exclusion amount. Having only one child is often the case these days, where there are two-career parents working full time.

A summary of the exclusion-versus-credit routes is presented in Figure 3.4. Do be aware that the $100,000 gross wages "dividing line" shown is suggestive on our part only. This dollar amount is not cast in statutory or regulatory concrete. Also be aware that there are distinct differences between the treatment of married filing separately in Part II (credit) and Part III (exclusion) on Form 2441.

When "Married Filing Separately"

Form 2441 is intended primarily for married persons who file joint returns. This intent is quite clear in Parts II and III. In both parts, the same two lines appear. These lines are—

- *Enter YOUR earned income* $_____
- *If married filing a joint return, enter YOUR SPOUSE'S earned income* $_____

The term "earned income" refers to personal services that you rendered to others that require your time and attention *away from* your child, children, or dependent(s). In other words, income derived from interest, dividends, capital gains, pensions, annuities, trusts, etc., although fully taxed, are not treated as earned income for purposes of Form 2441.

In the spousal line in Part II (credit), there is no preprinted mention whatsoever of "married filing separately." Said clause

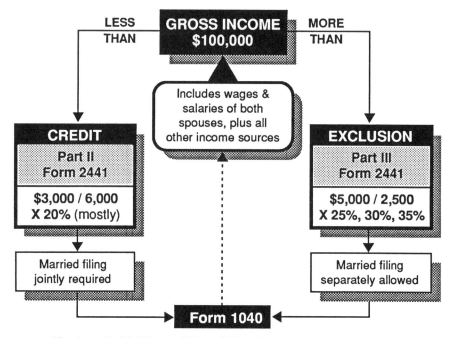

Fig. 3.4 - Quick "Rule of Thumb" for Best Option on Form 2441

appears in the spousal line in Part III (exclusion). It appears just below the line: *Enter your **earned income**,* and reads—

If married filing a separate return, see instructions for the amount to enter.

The pertinent instruction (accompanying Form 2441) is subheaded: ***Married Persons Filing Separate Returns***. It applies to both Parts II and III and reads—

*If your filing status is married filing separately and **all** of the following apply, you are **considered unmarried** for purposes of figuring the credit and the exclusion on Form 2441:*

- *You **lived apart** from your spouse during the last 6 months of ___[year]___ , and*

- *The qualifying person lived in your home more than half of*
  ___[year]___ , and

- *You provided over half the cost of keeping up your home.*

If you meet [these] *requirements to be treated as unmarried . . .,*
you may take the credit or the exclusion. If you do not meet all
of the requirements to be treated as unmarried, you **cannot** *take*
the credit. **However, you may take the exclusion.**

Part III points out, by inference, that, if you qualify as unmarried
and your spouse also qualifies as unmarried (implying two or more
dependents between the two of you), the maximum exclusion
benefit that you can claim is $2,500. The intent, obviously, is to
prohibit a married couple (living apart) claiming two $5,000
exclusions. If there is only one child, the custodial-parent rule
(below) governs who gets the $2,500 exclusion base.

What If Legally Unmarried?

The special tax rule above is called: "deemed unmarried." Such
is *not* the same as being legally unmarried. If one is divorced,
legally separated, widowed, head of household, or single, is Form
2441 not applicable? Are you deprived of the dependent-care credit
or exclusion, simply because of being legally unmarried?
Answer: No; you are not deprived of the credit or the exclusion.
That is, provided you meet certain qualifying conditions.
For an unmarried person, the qualifying conditions for the use
of Form 2441 are:

1. The care is provided so that you can work or look for work.
   But, if you cannot find a job and had no earned income for
   the year, you cannot use Form 2441.

2. You paid over half of the cost of keeping up your home for
   the claiming year: rent, mortgage, taxes, utilities, food, etc.

3. You and your qualifying person(s) lived in the same home.

4. The person who provided the care was not a person whom you claim as a dependent.

Under these conditions, the spousal line in Parts II and III are a duplicate of *YOUR earned income*. In particular, the last clause in the spousal line in Parts II and III says—

All others [who are unmarried], *enter the amount from* [your earned income] *line.*

In other words, when legally unmarried, the same maximum credit base ($3,000/$6,000) and/or the same maximum exclusion base ($5,000) applies, whether married or unmarried. There is a practical reason for this "no distinction" in marital status. The dependent-care credit/exclusion is a benefit to those who are working . . . and paying tax on their earned income(s). It is not a benefit that favors those who are married versus those who are not married. The credit/exclusion is strictly work related.

Children of Divorced Parents

In Chapter 2: Dependents & Exemptions, we have a section with the same subheading as above: "Children of divorced parents" (commencing on page 2-9). The discussion at that time was who could claim the dependency exemption: the custodial or the noncustodial parent. In essence, the custodial parent got the dependency exemption . . . unless. The "unless" is, if the custodial parent releases his/her claim to the dependency exemption via **Form 8332**, or a substitute, the noncustodial parent can claim the exemption deduction for that year. A Form 8332-type release is beneficial where the noncustodial parent makes child support payments (which are not taxable) to the custodial parent.

In this chapter, our focus has been on the dependent-care credit/ exclusion when expenses are paid to someone else, while the parent or parents are working. As you should know by now, the dependent-care credit/exclusion is a separate benefit independent of the dependency-exemption deduction. Ordinarily, a custodial parent can claim *both* benefits, if the qualifying conditions are met.

We now call to your attention another special rule, namely: Section 21(e)(5): *Special Dependency Test in Case of Divorced Parents, Etc.* The essence of this rule is that **if** the custodial parent releases his/her dependency exemption claim, the released child . . .

shall be treated as a qualifying individual . . . with respect to the custodial parent . . . and shall not be treated as a qualifying individual with respect to the noncustodial parent.

For this purpose, the "qualifying individual" must be—

under the age of 13 or physically or mentally incapable of caring for himself.

As depicted in Figure 3.5, Section 21(e)(5) is a clear splitting of the two dependency tax benefits: exemption vs. credit/exclusion. This "splitting arrangement" applies only to divorced or separated parents with minor children.

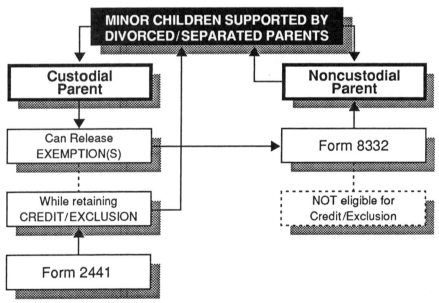

Fig. 3.5 - Effect of "Special Rule" for Children of Divorced Parents

The divorce/separation requirement is outlined in Section 152(e)(1): ***Custodial parent gets exemption.*** Where a child receives over half of his total support from both parents who—

(i) *are divorced or legally separated under a decree of divorce or separate maintenance, or*
(ii) *are separated under a written separation agreement, or*
(iii) *live apart at all times during the last 6 months of the calendar year, and*
(iv) *such child is in the custody of one or both parents for more than one-half of the calendar year,* [then]

such child shall be treated . . . as receiving over half of his support during the calendar year from the parent having custody for a greater portion of the year.

The whole point here is that minor children (those under age 13) of divorced or separated parents receive special consideration under the tax rules. This provides opportunity for the parents — at least for the sake of the children — to communicate with each other sensibly and try to work out a tax arrangement that is beneficial to each parent. This is often easier said than done. Mutuality of tax interests depends on the financial circumstances, the availability of a "home" for each child, and whether or not one parent or both have remarried, or intend to remarry.

4

THE CHILD TAX CREDIT

There Is A "Bonus" Tax Credit For Families With Dependent Children Under Age 17. The Credit Is $600 Per Child, PER YEAR (Ultimately Increasing To $1,000). The Actual Allowable Amount Is Subject To "Phaseout" For Incomes Over $110,000 (Married Filing Jointly), And To "Staging Rules" For Designated Intervening Credits. This Credit Is Unique In That It May Consist Of BOTH Nonrefundable And Refundable Components. The Nonrefundable Portion Requires That A WORKSHEET (In The Instructions) Be Prepared. The Refundable Portion Requires That A SPECIAL FORM: "Additional Child Tax Credit" Be Prepared.

In 1997, Congress enacted an entirely new child tax credit for children under age 17. In 2002, it increased substantially the dollar amount of the credit. For this credit, no expenditures for the care, well-being, education, or adoption of children are required. It is a pure tax credit simply for having children — and taking full responsibility for them — on your own. We think of it as a "bonus credit" for modest income families with children. For this credit, strategizing means using it whenever, and as often as, you can.

The child credit has a unique feature of its own. It has — or may have — both a nonrefundable component *and* a refundable component. The nonrefundable component applies only as an offset against your tentative tax. The refundable component applies — or may apply — to families with large itemized deductions who have two, three, or more children. In any case, the current credit is $600 per child . . . PER YEAR . . . increasing to $1,000 per child per year. This means that the credit may be claimed year after year, so long as a child has not attained age 17 during the year.

This credit, like most personal credits, is subject to phaseout rules. Generally, phaseout commences at $110,000 for married filing jointly; at $75,000 for single, head of household, or qualifying widow(er); and at $55,000 for married filing separately.

The nonrefundable portion of the child credit does *not* require the attachment of any special tax form to your return. You follow a "worksheet" computational procedure which you keep for your records. For the *refundable* portion, however, you prepare a second worksheet and then a Form 8812: *Additional Child Tax Credit*, which you attach to your return.

In this chapter, therefore, we want to apprise you of the basic tax law (IRC Sec. 24) authorizing this credit, who constitutes a qualified child, the credit distinction between modest income and low income families, how the nonrefundable and refundable credits are computed, and how the phaseout rules are applied. Helpful in this regard is a synopsis of page 2 of Form 1040. Such a synopsis establishes how the regular tax, nonrefundable credits, other taxes, and refundable credits relate to each other.

Overview of Section 24

Whenever a new tax law goes into effect, it is always best to overview that law so as not to be misled by hearsay misconceptions. You surely know by now that any new tax benefit authorized by Congress can be interpreted away by the IRS. As you'll see in a moment, Section 24 has some tax traps of its own. Because we are dealing with a bonus credit, it is the IRS's intent not to let this one credit alone eliminate all of your tax liability.

Section 24 is officially titled: *Child Tax Credit*. Its subsection (a): *Allowance of credit*, says—

*There shall be allowed as a credit against the tax imposed . . . for the taxable year with respect to each qualifying child of the taxpayer, an amount equal to the **per child** amount. [This] amount shall be . . . $600 [increased to] $1,000.*

With a statement like this, it sounds as though you had an absolute right to the $600 to $1,000 per-child per-year credit. As you'll see later, the traps to be cautious about are the terms: "tax imposed," "taxable year," and "qualifying child."

Other subsections and numbered paragraphs of Section 24 are—

Subsec. (b)   — Limitations
          (1)   Limitation based on adjusted gross income
          (2)   Threshold amount
          (3)   Limitation based on amount of tax
"   (c)   — Qualifying child
          (1)   Any dependent child
          (2)   Exception for certain noncitizens
"   (d)   — Portion of credit refundable
          (1)   Increased credits allowed
          (2)   Social security taxes
          (3)   Inflation adjustment
"   (e)   — Identification requirement
"   (f)   — Taxable year must be full taxable year

This last subsection, 24(f), is rather innocuous looking. Sounds like common sense. But what does that subsection really say?

It says—

Except in the case of a taxable year closed by reason of the death of the taxpayer, no credit shall be allowed under this section in the case of a taxable year covering a period of less than 12 months.

Yes, this is what the tax law says. But what does it really mean in terms of the child credit itself?

It means that if you have a qualifying child who reaches age 17 before the close of a calendar year, you are not allowed the credit for that child. For example, if your child became 17 on December 30, say, you get no bonus credit whatsoever. Furthermore, you do not even get a proration (363/365) of the credit. Any proration derives solely from the limitation rules of subsection (b) above.

Who is a Qualifying Child?

Subsection 24(c)(1) defines a qualifying child in tax law specifics. We prefer citing the instructions that accompany your Form 1040 re "Child Tax Credit." These instructions are much more straightforward than the wording in subsection 24(c)(1).

As per your Form 1040 instruction booklet—

A qualifying child is a child who:

- *Is claimed as a dependent on* [your return], ***and***

- *Was **under age 17** at the end of* [your calendar year], ***and***

- *Is your son, daughter, adopted child, grandchild, stepchild, or foster child,* ***and***

- *Is a U.S. citizen or resident alien.*

As with all dependents, a qualifying child must have, as his principal place of residence, your home, and he must be a member of your household. The idea is that it is costing you money to provide room and board, and it is expected that the child is taking advantage of your hospitality.

The Form 1040 instructions go on to say—

*A child placed with you by an authorized placement agency for legal adoption is an **adopted child** even if the adoption is not final.*

*A **grandchild** is any descendant of your son, daughter, or adopted child and includes your great-grandchild, great-great-grandchild, etc.*

*A **foster child** is any child you cared for as your own child and who lived with you for all of* [the taxable year]. *A child who was born or died* [during the current year] *is considered to have lived* *with you for all of* [the current year] *if your home was the child's home for the entire time he or she was alive.*

As you can sense, the definition of a child qualifying you for the $600 to $1,000 tax credit is almost identical with that for claiming a dependent on Form 1040. The difference is the age factor: the child must not have attained age 17 upon close of the taxable year.

If you will look at the dependency block (line **6c**: **Dependents**) on the front of your Form 1040, you will find a **column (4)**. As we depict in Figure 4.1, column (4) consists of a checkbox on each line for which you have entered: (1) the name, (2) SSN, and (3) relationship of each of your dependents. The column (4) is officially headed—

✓ *if qualifying child for child tax credit.*

If your adjusted gross income is less than $110,000 (married/joint), no formal attachment to your return is required. Your claim is automatically honored when your child's SSN is verified by the IRS. If above $110,000, the child tax credit begins to phase out. This means that only part of the credit may be allowed.

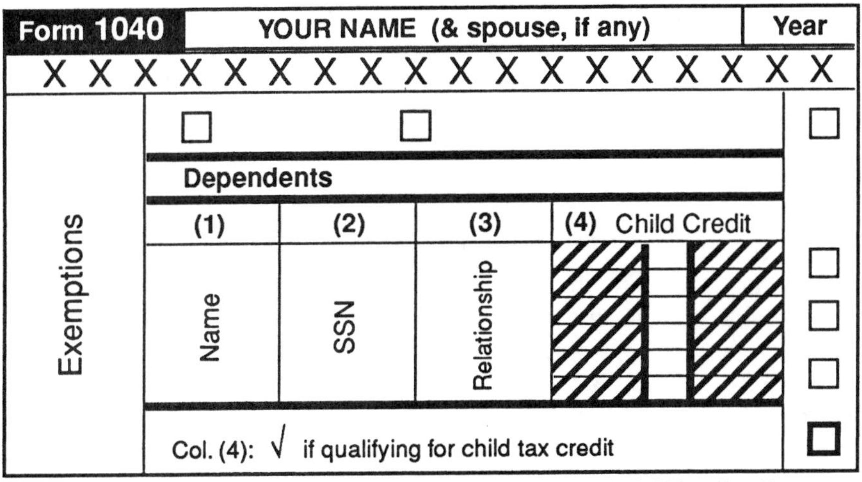

Fig. 4.1 - How to Indicate Under Age 17 for the Child Tax Credit

Use Worksheet for Phaseouts

If your adjusted gross income (AGI) exceeds statutory threshold amounts, there is a "phaseout" of the $600/$1,000 credit. The phaseout amount is $50 for each $1,000 or fraction thereof, in excess of your filing status threshold. The general phaseout rule is Section 24(b)(1): *Limitation Based on Adjusted Gross Income*:

*The amount of credit allowable under subsection (a) shall be reduced (but not below zero) by $50 for each $1,000 (or fraction thereof) by which the taxpayer's **modified** adjusted gross income exceeds the threshold amount.*

The prescribed threshold amounts are—

(A) $110,000 . . . for a married/joint return,
(B) $ 75,000 . . . for an individual not married, and
(C) $ 55,000 . . . for married filing separately.

The term *modified adjusted gross income* is your regular AGI "modified" by adding back any exclusions you may have claimed for foreign earned income, income from American Samoa, or income from Puerto Rico. Realistically speaking, these sources of exclusionary income would affect very few parents in the U.S. Therefore, your regular AGI applies. As the phaseout thresholds above imply, other calculations more directly affect your allowable child tax credit.

To do the phaseout calculation right, you have to use the worksheet in the instruction booklet accompanying Form 1040. This worksheet is titled: *Child Tax Credit Worksheet — Keep for your records.* Our abridgment of this worksheet is presented in Figure 4.2. Note that we have labeled Step 7 as: *Tentative allowable credit.* It is "tentative" in the sense that there are five other intervening credits before the child credit is subtracted from your regular tax.

A simple illustration of the phaseout calculation goes like this. Suppose, as a married person filing a joint return, your modified AGI is $125,000. Your phaseout amount would be:

```
///////  CHILD TAX CREDIT WORKSHEET    Do Not File
```

1. $600 x _____ -------------------------------- 1. _____
   Enter # of children under 17

2. Are you excluding foreign income?
   ☐ **No.** Enter regular AGI ⎫
   ☐ **Yes.** Enter modified AGI ⎭   **2.** _____

3. Enter for your filing status:
   • $110,000 - married joint   ⎫
   • $75,000 - unmarried   ⎬ **3.** _____
   • $55,000 - married separate ⎭

4. Is Step 2 more than Step 3
   ☐ **No.** Enter 0 here & at Steps 5 & 6 ⎫
   ☐ **Yes.** Subtract Step 3 from Step 2 ⎭ **4.** _____

5. Divide Step 4 by $1,000. --------------------- **5.** _____
   Round up to next whole #.

6. Multiply $50 by Step 5 ----------------------------- **6.** _____

7. **Tentative allowable credit** ------------------------- **7.** _____
   Subtract Step 6 from Step 1. If zero or less, **STOP.**

Note: $600 thru 2004; $700 thru 2008; $800 in 2009; $1,000 in 2010.

Fig. 4.2 - How Phaseout is Computed on Worksheet, Form 1040 Instructions

$$\frac{\$125,000 - \$110,000}{\$1,000} \times \$50 = \frac{15,000}{1,000} \times \$50 = \$750$$

You subtract this $750 phaseout from the $600 credit times the number of qualifying children you claim. Obviously, if you have only one such child, you get no credit whatsoever. If you have two children, your tentative credit would be $450 (600 x 2 – 750). If you have three children, your potential credit *might be* $1,050 (600 x 3 – 750). We say "might be," because other matters may intervene. For example, certain credits (such as education credits) take priority. Additionally, "threshold interference" may occur when claiming two different credits for the same child.

Other Intervening Credits

As stated earlier, the child tax credit is like a bonus. It is not a priority credit by any means. Other intervening nonrefundable credits take precedence in a prescribed staging order.

Actually, there are three intervening credit stages. They are characterized as: *Who Must Use Publication 972—*

Stage 1 — Are you excluding income from Puerto Rico, American Samoa, or are you filing Form 2555 (relating to working abroad)?

☐ No. *Continue.* ☐ Yes. *Must use Pub. 972.*

Stage 2 — Is your AGI on Form 1040 more than the phaseout amounts (previously listed)?

☐ No. *Continue.* ☐ Yes. *Must use Pub. 972.*

Stage 3 — Are you claiming any of the following credits?

- Adoption credit, Form 8839
- Mortgage interest credit, Form 8396
- District of Columbia first-time homebuyer credit, Form 8859

☐ No. Use simplified worksheet in instructions to Form 1040 to figure the credit, after subtractions (if any) for those intervening credits listed in Figure 4.3.

☐ Yes. *Must use Pub. 972.*

Publication 972: *Child Tax Credit,* consists of 15 pages of quite straightforward and helpful information. Its core approach is to have you step your way through various worksheets, depending on your income, filing status, and number of children. A

Form 1040	Based on Tax Year 2002	Page 2

Regular tax _____
Alternative minimum tax _____
Combined tax _____

1.	Foreign tax credit _____
2.	Dependent care credit _____
3.	Elderly / disabled credit _____
4.	Education credits _____
5.	Retirement savings credit _____
6.	**CHILD TAX CREDIT** _____
7.	Adoption credit _____
Etc.	Other credits (various) ☐ Personal _____ ☐ Business _____

Add all of the above: **Total Credits** ·················▶

Reduced Tax, but NOT below zero ·················▶

Fig. 4.3 - Listing of Key Nonrefundable Credits on Form 1040

subheading at each worksheet says: *Keep for your Records*. A careful reading of the instructions at each worksheet line is required. If you have one or more children under age 17, we highly encourage you to procure from the IRS a copy of its Publication 972. This publication is updated annually.

Nonrefundable vs. Refundable

At this point, it is instructive to digress for a moment to explain more directly the distinction between nonrefundable and refundable credits. Each type appears in separate portions of Form 1040: *U.S. Individual Income Tax Return* . . . on page 2. The credits preprinted on Form 1040 are not limited to those described in previous or subsequent chapters, nor to those described/listed in this chapter. What we have described or listed are personal credits. There are also business credits on page 2 of Form 1040.

All nonrefundable credits appear in the upper half of page 2, whereas the refundable credits appear in the lower half. Between these two functionally different credits, there are "other taxes" and "other payments." The first six lines of page 2 are devoted to the sequence for arriving at your regular income tax. As we have pointed out from time to time earlier, none of the credits has any effect until your regular tax has been established.

A "credit" is an offset, dollar-for-dollar, against your tax. More specifically, the term *nonrefundable* means that if you wipe out your tax, the unused portion of any remaining credit generally disappears. Exceptions apply to the child adoption credit and most business credits . . . which can be carried over to the following year(s).

In contrast, a *refundable* credit means that if the total of such credits exceeds your tax, the excess credits are paid to you as a refund. Because of this refundable nature, such credits are policed more stringently by the IRS. This is especially true when claiming the *additional* child tax credit.

To help you visualize, first hand, the sequence of tax computations involved, we present Figure 4.4. Our depiction is a generalized synopsis of what takes place on page 2 of Form 1040. It is not complete in every minutiae of detail, but you get the idea. Knowing the functionality aspects of page 2 can help you do a better job of strategizing for the lowest family tax possible. So, please take a moment to scan our figure 4.4.

Note at the line marked: *Regular tax*, there are two checkboxes, **a** and **b**. Have you ever noticed them before? Probably not. Unless you have children under 14 with significant investment income, or unless you are about to retire or have just retired, these checkboxes have no impact on your tax. Both checkboxes involve "add-ons" to your regular tax.

Additionally, as shown in Figure 4.4, there is another pervasive add-on tax. It is called **AMT**: *Alternative Minimum Tax*. We'll discuss this AMT matter in Chapter 11, later. Meanwhile, there is ongoing legislative "chatter" to the effect that the nonrefundable credits will not be allowed to diminish the AMT one iota. The rationale is that with so many personal and business tax credits available, there should be at least some minimum tax to be paid.

Form 1040	Individual Income Tax Return	Page 2

Computational Sequence

- Adjusted gross income, Standard deduction, OR Itemized deductions
- Personal exemptions

[Follow Instructions]

Taxable Income _____

Regular Tax - if applicable   **a** ☐ **b** ☐ ▬▬▬▬▬▬

Plus, also if applicable: Alternative minimum tax _____

Nonrefundable Credits

SEE FIG. 4.3

[SUBTRACT]

Total credits _____

Reduced Tax . . . . ▬▬▬▬▬▬

OTHER TAXES

- Self-employment   • Premature IRAs, etc.
- Soc. Sec. on tips   • Household employment

[ADD]

Total other taxes _____

Total Tax . . . . ▬▬▬▬▬▬

Refundable Credits

- Regular withholdings   • excess SS withheld
- Estimated prepayments   • Add'l child tax credit
- Earned Income Credit   • Extension payments

[SUBTRACT]

Total payments _____

YOUR YEAR-END STRATEGIZING GOAL	*REFUND OR* *AMOUNT DUE* → ☐

Fig. 4.4 - Block Functionalizing Selected Items on Page 2 of Form 1040

Also note in Figure 4.4 that we have highlighted the functional blocks designated as: Nonrefundable Credits, Other Taxes, and Refundable Credits. As should be obvious from its title, our primary focus in this book is on personal tax credits and on those opportunities for personal tax savings. There are also numerous (nearly 20) business-related tax credits. They are simply beyond the scope of this book. Furthermore, except for the refundable portion of the child tax credit, we have probably covered all that we intend to cover regarding personal refundable credits. Such refundable items as tax withholdings, estimated tax prepayments, payments with extension requests, and excess social security withholdings are self-explanatory to those in the habit of filing Forms 1040 regularly.

Refundable Portion of Credit

As a personal credit, the child tax credit is by far the single-most beneficial nonrefundable credit of all. For parents filing jointly with incomes up to around $130,000, it provides a truly substantial tax reduction. But, what happens at the other end of the family economic spectrum: say, incomes of less than $65,000? For these lower income families, what happens when the child and other credits wipe out the tax altogether?

Here's where the *additional* child tax credit — a refundable amount — comes into play. For this refundability, a separate entry line appears in the *Payments* block on page 2 of Form 1040. In said block, there is a total of nine payment credits which, when combined, often produce a refund check from the IRS. The particular caption of interest here reads—

Additional child tax credit. Attach Form 8812

Before we introduce Form 8812 to you, we need to present some background commentary.

In 2002, Congress materially altered the refundability of the child tax credit. Formerly, it applied only to low-income families (under $30,000) with three or more children. Now it applies to all filers (under certain conditions) as well as those with three or more qualifying children. These new law aspects are prescribed in Section 24(d): *Portion of Credit Refundable*. This is a 450-word tax law which is not clearly written.

To illustrate our lack-of-clarity point, the introductory wording to Section 24(d) reads (in part)—

The aggregate credits allowed to a taxpayer under [refundable credits] *shall be increased by* **the lesser of—**

(A) *the credit which would be allowed . . . without regard . . . to the limitation under subsection (b)(3)* [re the combined tax: regular plus AMT]*, or*

(B) *the amount by which the aggregate amount of credits allowed . . . would increase if the limitation imposed by subsection (b)(3) were increased by* **the greater of—**

    (i) *15 percent (10 percent . . . for taxable years beginning before 2005) of so much of the taxpayer's* **earned income** *. . . which is taken into account . . . as exceeds $10,000 or*

    (ii) *the credit allowed under Section 32* [re the Earned Income Credit] *for the taxable year.*

What basically takes place in Section 24(d) is the introduction of a new qualifying threshold for the child credit. You probably did not sense this on your own, even though we intentionally emphasized above the phrase "earned income." The new threshold is called: *Taxable Earned Income* (TEI). Such income — in contrast to adjusted gross income — is strictly personal service income on which social security and medicare taxes are paid. Included are wages, salaries, tips, commissions, self-employment income, and active partnership income. Excluded are interest, dividends, capital gains, rental income, and other passive sources of income and adjustments which constitute one's adjusted gross income (AGI). The role of TEI will become more clear when you acquaint yourself with **Form 8812**: *Additional Child Tax Credit.*

Abridgment of Form 8812

We had to cite and comment above so that you'd appreciate better the relative simplicity of Form 8812. It consists of just 13 computational line entries and four No-Yes checkboxes. It is arranged in three parts, namely:

Part I   — All Filers

Part II — Certain Filers Who Have Three or More Qualifying Children

Part III — Your Additional Child Tax Credit

Most of the 13 line entries are either self-explanatory or have self-guiding instructions thereto. The checkboxes are simple questions answerable either ☐ No or ☐ Yes. On this general note, we present in Figure 4.5 our abridgment of Form 8812. We just want you to get the general idea of its format. The official IRS form has far more self-guiding instructions than we show in Figure 4.5.

Form 8812	ADDITIONAL CHILD TAX CREDIT	Year

Part I   All Filers   [Up to about $150,000 income]

1	Enter amount from line 1 of **Worksheet** (in instructions)	1
2	Enter amount of **nonrefundable** credit claimed	2
3	Subtract line 2 from line 1. If zero, STOP	3
	- you cannot take the refundable credit	
4	Enter your taxable earned income	4
5	If line 4 more than $10,000	5
	- enter $10,000 & subtract from line 4	
6	Multiply line 5 by 10% and enter	6
	[15% starting year 2005]	

Part II   Certain Filers   [Up to about $50,000 income]

7	Enter **withheld** social security / medicare taxes	7
8	enter self-employment & tip taxes	8
9	Add lines 7 and 8	9
10	Enter amount of EIC claimed	10
11	Subtract line 10 from line 11. If zero or less, enter zero [-0-]	11
12	Enter **larger** of line 6 or line 11	12

Part III   Your Additional Credit

13	Enter **smaller** of line 3 or line 12	13

Fig. 4.5 - Simplified Version of Form 8812: Refundable Child Tax Credit

Part I is fairly straightforward. If your taxable earned income (defined above and on the back of the form) is more than $10,000, chances are you'll be eligible for some amount of *refundable* child tax credit. This is especially so, if, due to large itemized deductions, you were unable to claim the full nonrefundable amount.

Part II of Form 8812 is a bit more complicated. It targets low-income families (under $30,000) who are also claiming the earned income credit (EIC). The EIC is an entirely separate refundable credit of its own. If the EIC amount exceeds the total of all social security, medicare, self-employment, and railroad retirement taxes, the amount of additional child tax credit (CTC) is reduced. The idea here is that there is a trade-off between EIC and CTC. It is unlikely that many readers of this book would qualify for the EIC. The maximum EIC is about $4,000 for taxable earned income between $10,000 and $15,000. It disappears entirely for incomes between $30,000 and $35,000.

Example Use of Form 8812

For illustrating the use of Form 8812 (as abridged in Figure 4.5), assume that a married couple has three qualifying children under age 17. The husband earns $50,000 in wages; the wife takes care of the children. To this wage income, the couple derives $15,000 from interest, dividends, capital gains, and rentals. These sources plus the wages provide an AGI (adjusted gross income) of $65,000. Because of high mortgage payments, property taxes, and employee business expenses, their itemized deductions on Schedule A, Form 1040, total $45,000. How much nonrefundable CTC (child tax credit) do they get? How much *refundable* CTC, if any, do they get? Use the rules for tax year 2002. Assume no AMT (alternative minimum tax) for that year.

The allowable *non*refundable credit is limited to the amount of regular tax for the couple and their three children. Their personal exemptions amount to $15,000 (5 x $3,000 for 2002). To determine the tax, the taxable income for the five-member family must be computed. Said taxable income is—

AGI $65,000

Less
- Itemized deductions <45,000>
- Personal exemptions ≤15,000>

                5,000

Tax (married filing jointly) $ 500

The maximum possible CTC for three children (year 2002) is $600 per child x 3 children = $1,800 . . . whether nonrefundable or refundable.

Inasmuch as the parents' tax is only $500, the amount of nonrefundable credit is also only $500. This leaves $1,300 which would be lost altogether, were it not for Form 8812.

With Form 8812: *Additional Child Tax Credit*, how much of the unused $1,300 can be claimed refundable?

Even though Figure 4.5 is an abridgment, it is useful for illustration purposes. Following the line sequence in Part I of that figure, we have—

Line 1.	Maximum possible CTC	$ 1,800
Line 2.	Amount nonrefundable allowed	500
Line 3.	Subtract line 2 from line 1	1,300
Line 4.	Taxable earned income (wages)	50,000
Line 5.	Subtract $10,000 from line 4	40,000
Line 6	Multiply line 5 by 10%	4,000

[Below is not shown in Figure 4.5]

Next.   *Do you have three or more qualifying children?*

☐   *No. Skip Part II and enter the **smaller** of line 3 or line 6 on line 13.*

☐   *Yes. If line 6 is equal to or more than line 3, skip Part II and enter the amount on line 3 on line 13.*

Line 13.   Your *refundable* CTC is $ 1,300

The idea behind Form 8812 is this. If you are unable to claim all of your maximum potential CTC as a nonrefundable credit, you may be able to get the difference as a refundable credit. If, due to other intervening credits, the amount on line 2 is zero, you might even get a refund check for the entire CTC amount!

5

CHILD ADOPTION CREDIT

> The Adoption CREDIT Is Potentially $10,000 PER CHILD, With Or Without Special Needs. There Is No Tax Limit To The Number Of Adoptions That May Qualify. For Non-Duplicated Expenses, An EXCLUSION Up To $10,000 Is Also Possible Where Assistance Is Provided By Your Employer. Eligible Expenses Include Adoption Fees, Court Costs, Travel, Attorney Fees, Etc. All Credits And Exclusions Are Computed On Form 8839 Where Certain Limitation And "Phaseout" Rules Apply. Any Unused Credit Can Be Carried Forward Up To 5 Years. Any Unused Exclusion Is Taxable. Congress Materially Improved The Adoption Tax Benefits In 2002.

In 1996, Congress enacted two new sections of the IR Code directed expressly at the adoption of children. One such new law is Section 23: *Adoption Expenses (Allowance of Credit)*; the other new law is Section 137: *Adoption Assistance Programs (Exclusion)*. Whereas Section 23 offers a *credit* for adopting a child, Section 137 offers an *exclusion* for certain "assistance" by one's employer when adopting a child. Together, these two new laws are clearly intended to be incentives to those families without children who want children. In 2002, under the *Job Creation and Worker Assistance Act* (P.L. 107-147), Congress enhanced these adoption tax incentives quite substantially. Both domestic and foreign adoptions are allowed.

Three classes of adoptive children are designated. They are—

- Children *without* special needs;
- Children *with* special needs;
- Foreign-born children

In either case, the maximum allowable credit or exclusion is $10,000 per child. (Pre-2002, the amount was $5,000.) The $10,000 amount is a **per child** limitation. It is not a per year per child limitation as is the case for the child tax credit (in Chapter 4). There is no limit to the number of children who can be adopted — two or three or so.

In addition to the per child limitation, there is a parental income limitation. That is, the credit/exclusion benefits phase out for adjusted gross incomes in excess of $150,000 (married filing jointly). Compared to the pre-2002 threshold of $75,000, recent legislation has improved things quite a bit.

In this chapter, therefore, we want to provide you with a "good handle" on the essential features of Sections 23 and 137. We want to inform you of: (a) who are "eligible children" for adoption; (b) qualified adoption expenses; (c) employer-provided adoption assistance; (d) the phaseout of benefits; and (e) the carryforward of unused credits to subsequent years. In order to claim the credit and/or the exclusion, Form 8839: *Qualified Adoption Expenses*, must be used. Of course, we'll explain this form to you, including highlights that you might otherwise miss on your own.

Adoption Credit Overview

The adoption credit is set forth in IRC Section 23: *Adoption Expenses*. This section comprises about 2,000 words which are arranged into nine subsections: (a) through (i). Subsection (a): *Allowance of Credit*, consists of three paragraphs. Paragraph (1): *In General*, reads—

In the case of an individual, there shall be allowed as a credit against the tax . . . the amount of the qualified adoption expenses paid or incurred by the taxpayer.

Paragraph (2): *Year Credit Allowed*, reads—

The credit under paragraph (1) with respect to any expense [therewith] *shall be allowed . . .*

> *(A)* *in the year **following*** [that in] *which such expense is paid or incurred . . . **if before** such adoption becomes final, and*
> *(B)* *for the year in which the adoption becomes final . . .* [whether] *paid or incurred during or after the* [final] *year.*

The idea here is that the allowable credit is primarily contingent upon the adoption process for a chosen child being legally finalized.

Note above that paragraph (1) uses the term "qualified adoption expenses." Such expenses are defined in subsection (d)(1): *Definitions; Qualified Adoption Expenses,* as those which are—

reasonable and necessary adoption fees, court costs, attorney fees, and other expenses . . .

> *(A)* *which are directly related to, and the principal purpose of which is for **the legal adoption of an eligible child,*** [Emphasis added.]
>
> *(B)* *which are not incurred in violation of any State or Federal law or in carrying out any surrogate parenting arrangement,*
>
> *(C)* *which are not expenses in connection with the adoption by an individual of a child who is the child of such individual's spouse, and*
>
> *(D)* *which are not reimbursed under an employer program or otherwise.*

As is emphasized above, the basic thrust of subsection 23(d)(1) is the attainment of the *legal adoption* of an *eligible child.* This means that any directly related expenses that are incurred before the adoption is final are partially delayed and not fully credit-considered until after the adoption is final. Since not all adoption attempts are successful, any disappointment expenses that have been paid are "suspended" until an adoptive child is in hand. This, we submit, is within the meaning of the term "other expenses" which are directly related to the legal adoption of an eligible child.

Who is an "Eligible Child"?

Subsection 23(d)(2) defines an "eligible child" as—

Any individual who—

(A)   has not attained age 18, or

(B)   is physically or mentally incapable of caring for himself [regardless of age]

Additionally, subsection 23(d)(3) defines a "child with special needs" as—

Any child [under age 18] *if—*

(A)   a State has determined that the child cannot or should not be returned to the home of his parents.

(B)   such State has determined that there exists with respect to the child a specific factor or condition (such as ethnic background, age, or membership in a minority or sibling group, or the presence of factors such as medical conditions or physical, mental, or emotional handicaps) because of which . . . such child cannot be placed with adoptive parents without providing adoption assistance, and

(C)   such child is a citizen or resident of the U.S. [The term "U.S." includes the possessions of the U.S.; Section 2117(h)(3).]

When the adoption is that of a "foreign child," a special rule applies [Subsec. 23(e)]. This rule says that—

In the case of an adoption of a child who is not a citizen or resident of the U.S.,

> *(1)* *subsection (a)* [relating to the allowance of a tax credit] *shall not apply to any qualified adoption expense . . . until such adoption becomes final, and*

> *(2)* *any such expense paid or incurred before . . . the adoption becomes final shall be taken into account . . . as if such expense were paid or incurred during such* [adoption-final] *year.*

This overview tax law language makes it quite clear that there are three separate classes of eligible adoptees. One class addresses "any individual" (child or handicapped adult); another class addresses a "child with special needs"; and the third addresses a "foreign-born child." These separate classes provide a wide range of adoption opportunities for childless couples.

Credit is "Per Child" Amount

Subsection 23(b)(1): *Dollar Limitation*, says—

The aggregate amount of qualified adoption expenses . . . [allowable] *under subsection (a) for all taxable years with respect to the adoption of a child . . . shall not exceed $10,000.*

Some explanation is needed concerning the terms: "aggregate amount" . . . "for all taxable years." The term *aggregate amount* means the sum total of **all** qualified expenses paid or incurred before, during, and after the year in which the adoption becomes final. The term *for all taxable years* — for children without special needs — means those years **following** the years of expenditure, and during and after the year of final adoption. For foreign children, there is just one taxable year: when the adoption is final.

In the case of a special needs child, a special rule applies. Said rule is subsection 23(a)(3): *$10,000 Credit for Adoption of Child with Special Needs Regardless of Expenses.* Keep this latter term: "regardless of expenses" in mind. It will help you interpret the actual tax law wording (which we think is a little fuzzy).

In edited form, subsection 23(a)(3) reads—

In the case of an adoption of a child with special needs which becomes final during a taxable year, the taxpayer shall be treated as having paid during such [final] *year . . . an amount equal to the* [difference between] *$10,000 . . .* [and] *the adoption expenses actually paid or incurred . . . during such* [final] *taxable year and all prior taxable years.*

In other words, in the final year of adoption of a special needs child, if the actual total qualified expenses come to $7,500, for example, the adoptive parents *shall be treated* as having paid $2,500 of the $10,000 allowable credit. This is legislative recognition of the fact that special needs children require greater expenditures long after adoption, relative to adopted children without special needs.

As the term *adoption of a child* implies, the $10,000 limit is a **per child** limit. It is not an annual limit. The $10,000 amount covers all directly related expenses (travel, meals, lodging, medical exams, prosthetic devices, handrails, ramps, etc.) for any one child whose adoption is finalized. If, for example, the adoption process takes place over three (qualifying) years for which $12,500 has been expended, only the first $10,000 amount qualifies. Any excess over $10,000 is disallowed. We highlight this feature in Figure 5.1.

Other Credit Limitations

The up-to-$10,000 credit per adopted child is not an absolute grant. It is limited by three other adoption-sensitive rules. One is called the "AGI phaseout" rule [AGI for Adjusted Gross Income], the second is called the "No double benefit" rule, and the third is called the "Amount of tax" rule. We will touch on each of these momentarily, but will present more specifics later (when we discuss Form 8839: Qualified Adoption Expenses).

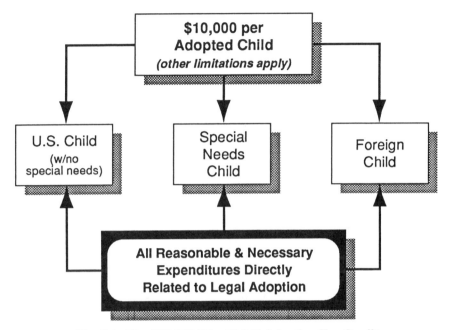

Fig. 5.1 - The $10,000 "Per Child" Adoption Tax Credit

The AGI phaseout rule is set forth in subsection 23(**b**)(**2**): *Income Limitation.* Its preamble wording is—

The amount allowable as a credit under subsection (a) for any taxable year . . . shall be reduced (but not below zero) by an amount which [is the] *ratio* [of]—

(Modified AGI – $150,000) ÷ $40,000

One's "modified" AGI is his regular AGI **increased** by any allowable exclusions for foreign earned income and U.S. Possessions income [Guam, Samoa, Puerto Rico, etc.].

The no-double-benefit rule is set forth in subsection 23(b)(3): *Denial of Double Benefit.* Its essence is—

No credit shall be allowed under subsection (a) for any expense—

> *(A)   For which a deduction or credit is allowed under any other provision for* [Normal Taxes and Surtaxes].
>
> *(B)   To the extent that funds for such expense are received under any Federal, State, or local* [assistance] *program.*

The idea here, of course, is that the allowable expenses are restricted to only those paid or incurred directly by the adoptive parents out of their own pockets.

The amount of tax limitation rule is set forth in subsection 23(b)(4): *Limitation Based on Amount of Tax.* It reads:

> *The credit allowed under subsection (a) for any taxable year* **shall not exceed** *the excess of—*
>
> *(A)   the sum of the regular tax liability . . . plus the* [Alternative Minimum Tax: AMT], *over*
>
> *(B)   the sum of* [all other personal] *credits allowed.*

In other words, the adoption credit is the "bottom rung" of the credits allowed, after all other personal credits intervene.

Because of the bottom-rung position of the adoption credit, Congress has empowered it with one truly unique feature. If the credit allowable for a given year exceeds the residual tax (after other credits), the unused portion can be carried forward through the next five years [Subsection 23(c)].

Employer-Provided Assistance

As part of the overall allowability of adoption expenses, there is directly related to Section 23 another supporting tax law. Said law is Section 137: *Adoption Assistance Programs.* This law authorizes an employer to adopt a qualified plan from which payments therefrom are *excluded* from an employee's gross income. On this point, subsection 137(a): *Exclusion,* expressly states—

> *Gross income of an employee* **does not include** *amounts paid or expenses incurred by the employer for qualified adoption*

expenses in connection with the adoption of a child by an employee if such amounts are furnished pursuant to an adoption assistance program. [Emphasis added.]

Thus, the key question here is: What is an "adoption assistance program"?

Subsection 137(c) defines such a program as—

a separate written plan of an employer for the exclusive benefit of such employer's employees—

> *(1) under which the employer provides such employees with adoption assistance, and*

> *(2) which meets* [certain] *requirements.*

The key "certain" requirement is that the plan be nondiscriminatory and that not more than five percent of the aggregate total benefits under the plan be payable to the owner(s) of the business.

The maximum excludable-from-income assistance amount . . .

for all taxable years with respect to the adoption of a child . . . shall not exceed $10,000 [Subsec. 137(b)(1)].

The kinds of adoption assistance expenditures are the same types as those which qualify under Section 23: Allowance of Credit. All other conditions and limitations described earlier for the $10,000 credit apply equally to the $10,000 exclusion amount. So, why are there two laws?

Answer: Under the right circumstances, both the $10,000 credit **and** the $10,000 exclusion may be claimed. The "right circumstances" are that there be no duplication or overlapping of claims for the same expenditures. This is called the "coordination princple" between the two laws. Let us explain.

Meanwhile, though, we present in Figure 5.2 the fundamental differences between Sections 23 and 137.

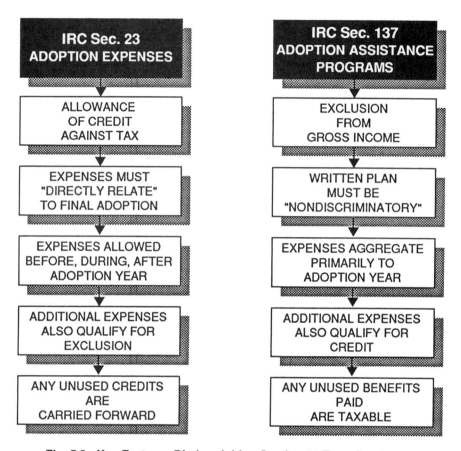

Fig. 5.2 - Key Features Distinguishing Section 23 From Section 137

Credit "and/or" Exclusion

Sections 23 and 137 permit a unique "coordination" of credit *and* exclusion benefits. In the legislative history of Section 137, Congress pointed out that—

*Adoption expenses paid or reimbursed under an adoption assistance program may not be taken into account in determining the adoption credit. A taxpayer may, however, satisfy the requirements of the adoption credit **and** exclusion* *with **different expenses** paid or incurred by the taxpayer and employer respectively.* [Emphasis added.]

This different-expenses ("and/or") concept is reinforced by **IRS Notice 97-9** (1997-1 CB 365) under its section: ***Coordination of Credit and Exclusion***. The lead-off paragraph: *Credit or Exclusion*, reads—

*An individual may claim **both** a credit and an exclusion in connection with the adoption of an eligible child. An individual may not, however, claim both a credit and an exclusion for the same expenses. For example, assume that* [a married couple] *pays $12,500 in qualified adoption expenses to an adoption agency for the final adoption of an eligible child who is not a child with special needs. In the same year,* [one of the spouse's] *employer, under an adoption assistance program . . . pays an additional $10,000 for other qualified adoption expenses to a private attorney on behalf of the employee for the adoption of the child. . . . Assuming that the couple's modified AGI is $150,000 or less, the individual may exclude $10,000 from gross income, **and** may claim a credit of $10,000 because the exclusion and credit are **not for the same expenses**. The remaining $2,500 of qualified adoption expenses may never be claimed as a credit or excluded from gross income.* [Emphasis added.]

This is a unique concept. For most adoption processes, so long as your expenditures are "directly related" thereto, and are not duplicates of each other, you can claim both the credit and the exclusion in the same year. There is no mutual exclusivity as in the case of the dependent-care credit/exclusion in Chapter 3.

Make Claim on Form 8839

To compute and claim the adoption credit and/or assistance exclusion, **Form 8839** must be used. This form is titled: ***Qualified Adoption Expenses***. We strongly urge that you get an official copy of this form from the IRS. It involves working your way through 30 computational lines, 10 of which are duplicated for each child.

This is because the $10,000 maximum credit or exclusion is a *per child* amount. A single Form 8839 only shows spaces for Child 1 and Child 2. Instructions accompanying the form say—

If you adopted or tried to adopt more than two eligible children, fill in and attach as many Forms 8839 as you need to list them.

Form 8839 is arranged into three parts:

Part I   — *Information about Your Eligible Child or Children*

Part II   — *Adoption Credit.* **Caution:** *If you received* **employer-provided adoption benefits,** *complete part III next.*

Part III   — *Employer-Provided Adoption Benefits*

Much of Form 8839 is self-explanatory due to preprinted instructions directly on its face. The form is accompanied by approximately 4,000 words of separate instructions and worksheets. Instructional complications arise when you start the adoption process a year (or two) before the adoption is final; or when one adoption fails and you start another; or when there is a foreign child adoption. Part I carries the subheading: *You must complete this part.*

As shown in Figure 5.3, Part I consists of two lines: Child 1 and Child 2. If you have Child 3 or Child 4, you prepare (and attach) another Form 8839. Whatever the number of eligible children involved, the child lines are columnized as follows:

Col. (a)   — Child's name; first, last
"   (b)   — Child's year of birth
"   (c)   — Child 18 or over and disabled
"   (d)   — Child with special needs
"   (e)   — Foreign child
"   (f)   — Child's Tax ID

Columns (e) and (f) require further explanation.

Form 8839	Qualified Adoption Expenses				Year

Before you begin, see Instructions for the meaning of
• Eligible Child • Employer-Provided Benefits • Qualified Expenses

Part I	Information about Eligible Child or Children				
(a)	**(b)**	Check if child was -			**(f)**
Child's name first, last	Year of birth	**(c)** Over 18 disabled	**(d)** Special needs	**(e)** Foreign child	Child's Tax ID
Child 1		☐	☐	☐	
Child 2		☐	☐	☐	
Add Another Form 8839					
Child 3		☐	☐	☐	
Child 4		☐	☐	☐	

Fig. 5.3 - Part I of Form 8839: The Part You "Must" Complete

There are always complications when adopting a foreign child. Most of the "complications" are benefit disqualifications and benefit delays. The credit (Part II) or exclusion (Part III) benefits do not materialize until the year the adoption is final. Any otherwise-qualified adoption expenses paid or incurred before the adoption is final are disqualified (though "suspended") for credit purposes. Any employer-provided assistance before the adoption is final is *taxable* (though "may be" picked up later). Consequently, the separate instruction to column (e) must be read and followed when a foreign adoption is in process.

Column (f), Part I, is paperwise more complicated than the column heading suggests. Not every prospective adoptive child has a Tax ID. Newborns and infants rarely ever do. For all adoptees, one of *three* types of ID must be acquired. They are:

SSN — Social Security Number. Use **Form SS-5.**
ATIN — Adoption Taxpayer Identification Number. Use **Form W-7A.**
ITIN — Individual Taxpayer Identification Number. Use **Form W-7.**

[**Form SS-5**: Application for a Social Security Card; **Form W-7A**: Application for Taxpayer Identification Number for Pending U.S. Adoptions; **Form W-7**: Application for IRS Individual Taxpayer Identification Number.] You can get these forms (as well as Form 8839) by calling 1-800-TAX-FORM (1-800-829-3676). The IRS will not process your Form(s) 8839 if there is no entry in column (f) of Part I.

Separate Computation: Each Child

In Part II (credit), there are five "starting lines" of computation. Similarly, in Part III (exclusion) there are five such lines. Three of these starting lines — we'll call them "steps" — are identical in Parts II and III. Two of the five steps are not identical (though comparable). The similarities of these starting steps in Parts II and III derive from the fact that each computational entry pertains to one child at a time. Earlier, we pointed out that the maximum allowable credit and/or exclusion is a *per child* limit. Consequently, whether you have two or more adoptions being processed simultaneously or sequentially, the allowable amount of credit and/or exclusion will differ for each child.

For instructional convenience, we portray in Figure 5.4 the five starting steps for each child, for Parts II *and* III, alongside of each other. On an official Form 8839, Part II is on the front page; Part III is on the back page. If you haven't already done so, and you have an adoptive child in process, we urge that you get (from the IRS) an official form and its instructions.

Note in Figure 5.4 that Steps 1, 3, and 5 are identical in Parts II and III. We have abbreviated the wording at those steps. The official wording is on Form 8839 itself.

Step 2 (in Figure 5.4) while not identical in Parts II and III is functionally comparable. Each refers to your previous-year claims and benefits. Specifically, Parts II and III ask as follows:

Part II, Step 2	Part III, Step 2
Did you file a [prior year] *Form 8839?*	*Did you receive employer-provided adoption benefit for* [prior year]*?*

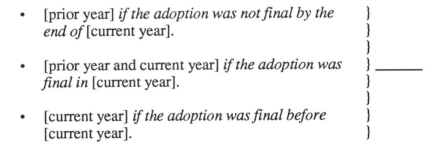

Fig. 5.4 - Parts II and III: Side by Side "Per Child" Comparison

The table shown in Fig. 5.4 (Abridgement of Form 8839: Front & Back pages):

Part II Adoption Credit	Child 1	Child 2	Part III Adoption Exclusion	Child 1	Child 2
1 Enter $10,000			1 Enter $10,000		
2 Prior credit claimed SEE TEXT			2 Prior benefit received SEE TEXT		
3 Subtract Step 2 from Step 1			3 Subtract Step 2 from Step 1		
4 Qualified Expenses paid in - • prior year • adoption year • current year			4 Employer benefit received in current year: Code T (Box 12) on W-2		
5 Enter SMALLER of Step 3 or Step 4			5 Enter SMALLER of Step 3 or Step 4		

[If] *No. Enter -0-.*   [If] *No. Enter -0-.*

[If] *Yes. See instructions for amount* [If] *Yes. See instructions for*
to enter.   *amount to enter.*

The key computational differences between Parts II and III emanate from Step 4 (in Figure 5.4). Part II, **Step 4** states—

Enter the total qualified adoption expenses you paid in:

• [prior year] *if the adoption was not final by the end of* [current year].

• [prior year and current year] *if the adoption was final in* [current year].

• [current year] *if the adoption was final before* [current year].

In contrast to the above, the **Step 4** in Part III directs you to—

Enter the total amount of employer-provided adoption benefits received in [current year]. *This amount should be shown in Box 12 of your* [current year] *W-2 form(s) with code T.*

In Part II, you are given more latitude in accumulating your expenditures for the credit than in Part III for employer assistance. Except for special needs domestic adoptions, you are pretty well limited in employer assistance to the year in which the adoption becomes final. It is a matter of knowing at that time the extent of your actual expenditures. Therefore, for strategizing purposes, you pay all expenses before and after the adoption year. Then have the employer pay them — if he has a qualified plan for doing so — for the adoption year. Any excess adoption-year costs can be paid and claimed by you as part of your Part II computation. This, we believe, will give you your best chance at claiming *both* the credit and the exclusion.

When Benefits "Phase Out"

Both the adoption credit and the adoption exclusion are subject to an income "means test." If your income is below $150,000, there is no means testing. If your income is $190,000 or higher, the credit and exclusion — for that taxable year — "phase out" in their entirety. For incomes between $150,000 and $190,000, the phaseout rules of Section 23(b)(2) [for the Part II credit] and Section 137(b)(2) [for the Part III exclusion] apply.

More correctly, the term "income" here refers to your *modified adjusted gross income* (or modified AGI). Your modified AGI is your regular AGI (bottom of page 1 of Form 1040) PLUS *any and all exclusions* not included in your regular AGI. Since the phaseout is a means test, the addback of your exclusions (such as the adoption exclusion, dependent care exclusion, etc.) does not increase your regular income tax. The addbacks simply increase the magnitude of your phaseout fraction. When this fraction increases, your credit and exclusion are reduced.

The statutory wording of Sections 23(b)(2) and 137(b)(2): *Income Limitation*, is comprehensively too awkward. Giving you the formula makes better sense. The formula is—

Phaseout fraction $= \dfrac{\text{Modified AGI} - \$150{,}000}{\$40{,}000}$

$= 0.\underline{\hspace{1cm}}$ (rounded to at least 3 decimals)

This formula is "built into" Form 8839 in Parts II and III.

For a numerical illustration of how the phaseout rule works, consider a married couple with a modified AGI of $172,500. They paid $8,000 to an adoption agency for a special needs child; their employer paid $10,000 to an adoption attorney for the same child. The adoption became final in the year that these expenditures were made. What is the phaseout fraction, and what effect does the phaseout have in Part II and Part III of Form 8839?

The phaseout fraction is—

$\dfrac{172{,}500 - 150{,}000}{40{,}000} = 0.5625$

The phaseout reduction in Part II is 0.5625 x $8,000 = $4,500. Therefore, the *potentially* allowable credit is $8,000 – $4,500 or $3,500. We say "potentially" because other intervening credits may take priority.

The phaseout reduction in Part III is 0.5625 x $10,000 = $5,625. Therefore, the allowable exclusion is $10,000 – $5,625 or $4,375. Because the employer entered $10,000 in Box 12 (Code **T**) of the couple's W-2 form, the $5,625 nonexclusion amount becomes a taxable benefit on the *Wages, salaries* line of Form 1040. They so indicate by hand entering the letters "AB" (for Adoption Benefit) alongside of the $5,625.

Unused Credit Carryforwards

We mentioned previously that there was a unique feature to the adoption *credit*. Any allowable but unused portion can be carried forward to subsequent years. (There is no carryforward of any usable adoption exclusion benefits; that which is not usable, is taxable.)

The **credit** carryforward is expressly authorized by Section 23(c): *Carryforwards of Unused Credit.* The essence of this tax law is—

> *If the credit allowable under subsection (a) for any taxable year exceeds the limitation imposed by subsection (b)(4) for such taxable year, such excess shall be carried to the succeeding taxable year and added to the credit allowable under subsection (a) for such taxable year. No credit may be carried forward under this subsection to any taxable year following the fifth taxable year after the taxable year in which the credit arose.*

Let's cast this statutory language in better light. Suppose, for example, that you have a credit carryforward from two preceding (origin) years which totals $8,685. You have adopted two children without special needs. Your maximum potential credit at this point was $20,000 but you were only able to use $11,315 (20,000 − 8,685). In the current origin year, you are adopting a special needs child. This brings your maximum cumulative credit potential to $30,000 . . . for three adoptees. Your current year's unused credit — *after* any phaseout fraction — is $3,315. Altogether, now, you have $12,000 of credit carryforward (8,685 + 3,315) out of an initial $30,000 credit base.

Now, keep this easy-to-forget point in mind. Once a credit carryforward is determined in Part II of Form 8839 for a given origin year, it is no longer subject to any phaseout reductions. That is, the phaseout reduction is applied *only once*: in the year the credit is generated. It is not reapplied in subsequent years to reduce the credit carryforwards.

All of which means that each credit carryforward must be identified separately for each origin year. Thus, if you have three origin years, for example, year 1 is carried forward and used first. Year 2 is next carried forward, and year 3 is next. This way, you get the benefit of eight carryforward years, instead of just five years.

6

WEIGHING THE "NANNY TAX"

> If You Engage A HOUSEHOLD EMPLOYEE To Oversee
> The Care And Well-Being Of Your Children And Other
> Dependents, A New Tax Liability Is Imposed:
> EMPLOYMENT TAX. This Consists Of Social Security
> Taxes, Medicare Taxes, Unemployment Taxes, And
> Income Tax Withholdings (In Certain Cases). For
> Federal Purposes Only, Schedule H (Form 1040) Is
> Useful And Convenient. Unfortunately, Some States —
> California, Particularly — Ignore Schedule H And
> Impose Their Own Employment Tax Rules And Forms.
> State Aggressiveness May Cause You To Search For
> Alternative Arrangements With NONEMPLOYEES.

There is a downside to the child-and-dependent-care tax credit and exclusion benefits. There is — or could be — an applicable household employment tax, known as the "Nanny Tax."

If you have minor children or disabled adults in your household, you probably have engaged — or are considering engaging — someone to oversee their care and well-being. The "overseer" is an individual who is present in your home while you are out of the home being gainfully employed. You pay the overseer an hourly, daily, weekly, or monthly compensation.

Once the amount of compensation (in a given year) exceeds $1,200 for any one overseer, you have crossed the threshold into a completely new tax liability domain. You have now become a household **employer**. You have become such, whether you intended to or not. This means that there are household *employment taxes* to self-assess and pay.

What kind of employment taxes are we talking about?

For starters, there are *social security taxes* that you pay, as an empoyer of household employees. There are *medicare taxes* that you also pay. There are federal unemployment taxes, state unemployment taxes, and state disability insurance . . . that you pay. If the household overseer so requests, and you agree, there are income taxes to collect and pay over to the IRS (and to corresponding state agencies).

All of these taxes, collectively, can range from a low of $200 to a high of $1,500 per overseer. BUT, as you'll see below, the tax forms and tax accounting required of you become another headache and irritant in your otherwise busy life. Are there other options that you can pursue and weigh? Yes, there are.

In this chapter, therefore, we want to explain the types of persons who are classed as household employees, the federal tax law on point (IRC Sec. 3510), the IRS forms involved (Schedule H, Forms W-2 and W-3, Form 1099-MISC, etc.), the role of nanny service providers (some do all of the tax accounting), the role of child care and elderly care centers outside of your home, family members being overseers, and other arrangements that you might make to minimize the extra tax burdens placed upon you when there are workers in and around your home. Obviously, if you can do without such persons, you would be better off. Yet, there comes a time when you must factor into your strategizing plans your role as an employer of other persons taking care of your dependents.

Household Employees Defined

What types of persons are classed by the IRS as household employees? Those who perform services IN OR AROUND HOUR HOME. You requested that they perform the services. You expect to pay — and they expect to receive — adequate compensation therewith.

When you engage someone to perform household work, you tell him or her *what* you want, *when* you want it, and *how* you want it done. You provide the tools, supplies, and other items they need to perform the tasks intended. The fact that you may allow the worker wide latitude in the "what, when, and how" makes no difference. As a homedweller, you always have the right to control the details of any work performed in or around your home.

As a very simple example, suppose you are a single parent who engages an 18-year-old babysitter to watch your infant child while you are at work. In addition, you assign the sitter some light housekeeping duties. The sitter works four days a week, three months at a time, in and out of your home. You provide all of the necessary items for the care and well-being of your child This sitter is definitely your employee. However, if you engaged a sitter who was *under* 18 years of age, and was a student at an accredited educational institution nearby, such person would not be your employee. She would be occupationally classed as a "student."

Other persons working in or around your household who are considered employees are—

Caretakers	Eldersitters	Housekeepers
Cleaning people	Food preparers	Private nurses
Drivers	Health aides	Yard workers
. . . etc.		

If a worker is your employee, it does not matter whether the services are performed part time or full time, or that you engaged the worker through the Internet, a newspaper, an agency, or some volunteer arrangement. Nor does it matter that the compensation was paid by the hour, day, week, or job.

Employer taxes come into play only for *Cash Wages* paid. This is the specific term used when preparing the federal form: *Household Employment Taxes*. The term includes only those amounts paid in cash (green paper), personal check, or money order. The term "cash wages" does **not** include food, lodging, clothing, transportation (up to $65 per month), or other noncash items provided. The noncash is not taxable to the recipient because it is regarded as furnished for an employer's convenience. That is, for *your* convenience. It is the cash portion only that you pay Federal employment taxes on. If the workers you engaged were nonemployees, there would be no such taxes to pay.

Who Are Nonemployees?

We have already given you a hint that certain persons are IRS-classed as *nonemployees*. What was the hint? It was that under-18-year-old babysitter who was a student.

In general terms, the IRS (and many state employment taxing agencies) regard the following six categories of workers as nonemployees. Those so categorized are:

Group I — Any person under age 18 who is not ordinarily engaged in providing household services as his or her principal occupation. (Some states set this age at 16.)

Group II — Any student under age 24 enrolled in a full-time curriculum of academic instruction and work experience at a regularly organized educational institution. (Some states set this age at 22.)

Group III — Family members: your own child or children if under age 21 (some states say 18); your spouse; your parent(s), and your spouse's parent(s).

Group IV — Workers you hire through a temporary employment agency, if that agency takes on the role of an employer and contracts with you the scope and nature of the household chores to be performed.

Group V — Workers in a licensed day care, pre-school, after-school, week-end camp, or elder care center to which your dependents are transported to the care-providing facility, and returned to your home at the end of each ordinary work day. These persons are not your employees for the simple reason that their services are rendered entirely outside of your household domain. You have no control over the daily routine.

Group VI — Self-employed persons who work for others as well as for you, who are "in business for themselves," with whom you contract for services, and who provide their own tools, supplies, transportation, insurance, and other items necessary for accomplishing the contract you entered into. Such persons are more commonly called: *independent contractors.*

In theory, therefore, if you watched your Ps and Qs carefully, you could maneuver through the employment tax minefield . . . for many years. To do so would require that you know the exact age, attributes, and self-reliant status of each person that you hire. You would have to be prepared for a continuous turnover of such persons, and you would need an ongoing source of replacement workers. If you have normal children (not disabled or handicapped) and no senile parents to take care of, bypassing the employee role could work out. But do not count on this approach being a smooth ride. We'll point out specific pitfalls after we explain your tax duties as a household employer.

Rationale of Section 3510

In 1994, Congress passed the Social Security Domestic Employment Reform Act. The more functional title associated with this Act (P.L. 103-387) was: *Simplification of Employment Taxes on Domestic Services.* The end tax law result was IRC Section 3510: *Collection of Domestic Service Employment Taxes.* This new Section 3510 became effective for all taxable years commencing in 1995 and thereafter.

As is often the case with new tax laws, Congress held public hearings on the household employment tax situation. Testimony was offered by several high-profile political appointees who had not paid their nanny taxes for years and years. They pointed out that the former law which applied to all employers operating an ongoing business was inappropriate when applied to remuneration for domestic services in a private home. They testified that the law was absurd when applied to school-age children who rarely worked more than a few days or a few weeks at a time.

The absurdity of the former law was stressed by citing the low remuneration threshold for triggering the employment tax obligations. That threshold was $50 per calendar quarter (every three months). In other words for cash payments as low as $200 per year ($50/qtr x 4) to each worker, a household employer had to file five employment tax returns each year (one for each of four quarters, plus an annual return), plus the preparation of Form W-2 for each alleged employee. For a $200-per-year worker, the amount of employment tax payable to the IRS was around $40 (plus about $10 payable to state employment tax agencies). The IRS collects over 1.5 *trillion* dollars ($1,500,000,000,000) annually . . . and is troubled when it doesn't collect $50 from every 15-year-old babysitter? What a petty tax matter! The irritation and aggravation of the paperwork necessary for paying such a piddling amount of tax resulted in most household heads ignoring it. Only those in the political limelight at certain times were ever "caught" not paying the nanny tax. Most others ignored the employment tax issue altogether.

Nevertheless, Congress felt domestic workers should not be deprived of their right to social security, medicare, and unemployment benefits when the need arose. In its Committee Reports on the rationale for the new law, Congress said—

The provision [new law, Section 3510] *would simplify and streamline the payment of employment taxes on domestic workers, reducing significantly the administrative burden on their employers; eliminate liability for Social Security tax in cases where domestic employment is occasional or of short duration; and establish new enforcement mechanisms to improve domestic employers' tax compliance, thus insuring that workers receive the Social Security,* [Medicare]*, and Unemployment coverage to which they are entitled.*

Achieving these Congressionally directed provisions is what Section 3510 is all about.

Highlights of Section 3510

The full text of Section 3510 consists of about 550 words. This number is exclusive of its 13-word title which reads: *Coordination of Collection of Domestic Service Employment Taxes With Collection of Income Taxes.* Here, the term "coordination" refers to combining the payment of employment tax for domestic workers with your paying your own personal income tax. Any income tax of the domestic worker is a separate matter.

Section 3510 is one of those rare tax laws where, except for its general rule (always subsection (a)), the subsection headings are highly informative on their own. To illustrate our point, subsections (b) through (f) are titled:

Subsec. (b) — Domestic service employment taxes subject to estimated tax provisions.
" (c) — Domestic service employment taxes defined.
" (d) — Exception where employer liable for other employment taxes.
" (e) — General regulatory authority (re "coordination" with employers' income taxes).
" (f) — Authority to enter into agreements to collect state unemployment taxes.

These title headings give you the general idea of what to expect within each subsection. Subsections (a), (b), (c), and (f) have separately numbered paragraphs.

We add to the above headings a few amplifying comments of our own. Read subsection (b) as meaning that you must anticipate what your domestic worker's total employment taxes for the year will be, then up your own tax withholdings (or estimated prepayments) to cover that amount. Subsection (c) means that social security, medicare, and unemployment tax for each domestic worker is the "employment tax" that you pay. You may include the worker's income tax, if you and he/she agree to your withholding from him/her. Subsection (d) means that, if you conduct a regular trade or business, and you have nondomestic workers, you can include your domestic worker employment taxes along with those that you pay for your nondomestic workers. This means that you pay all employment taxes on a quarterly basis.

The *General Rule*, subsection (a), reads principally as—

Except as otherwise provided in [the subsections above]—

(1) *returns with respect to domestic service employment shall be made on a calendar year basis,*

(2) *any such return . . . shall be filed on or before . . .* [April 15th] *following the close of the employer's taxable year . . ., and*

(3) *no requirement to make deposits* [with authorized Federal Depository Institutions] *. . . shall apply with respect to such taxes.*

In brief, Congress has tried to make the imposition and collection of household employment taxes — the Nanny Tax — as unburdensome as possible. The central idea is to pay the domestic worker tax, along with your own income tax, each year. Many states join with the Federal government for collection of their state's unemployment taxes. Other states have their own separate employment tax process. In a state like California, the employment tax process is far more burdensome than it is for the Federal.

Schedule H (Form 1040)

The "coordination" that the IRS has done has been to design and prepare instructions to a Schedule H (Form 1040). The "H" is for *Household*. This special schedule is fully titled:

Household Employment Taxes
(For Social Security, Medicare, Withheld Income,
and Federal Unemployment Taxes)

▶ *Attach to* [your] *Form 1040 . . .* [etc.]

If you will look at the "Other Taxes" block on page 2 of your Form 1040 (or wish to glance back at our Figure 4.3 at page 4-10), you'll see that the last entry line in that block is captioned: *Household employment taxes. Attach Schedule H.* This is the tax — the Nanny Tax — that you pay for the privilege of having overseers of your dependents working in your home, under your control.

Schedule H is arranged into four separate blocks of information. Said blocks are:

☐ Threshold Questions: A, B, and C   }
                                             } Page 1
Part I   — Social Security, Medicare, & Income Taxes }

Part II   — Federal Unemployment (FUTA) Tax }
             (including State unemployment tax) } Page 2
Part III — Total Household Employment Taxes }

Needless to say, if you do have household employees, we urge that you get an official copy of Schedule H and its eight pages of instructions from the IRS. Otherwise, we touch only on selected highlights of the form.

In the upper half of Schedule H, there are three threshold questions. As edited, they read—

A. *Did you pay **any one** household employee cash wages of $1,200 or more during the year _____ ?*
☐ *Yes.* ☐ *No.*
B. *Did you withhold Federal income tax during _____ for any household employee?*
☐ *Yes.* ☐ *No.*
C. *Did you pay **total** cash wages of $1,000 or more in **any** calendar quarter of _____ to household employees?*
☐ *Yes.* ☐ *No.*

At each Yes-No that you check, there are preprinted instructions as to which line numbers (totaling 25) you make specific entries onto. For your overview convenience, we display in Figure 6.1 the general arrangement of Part I and Part II of Schedule H. Part III is a

Sch. H (Form 1040)	HOUSEHOLD EMPLOYMENT TAXES	Year

Threshold Questions: ☐ Yes ; ☐ No

Part I	Social Security, Medicare, & Income Taxes

1. **Total cash wages to all employees**
2. **Social security taxes**
   Multiply line 1 by 12.4% (0.124)
3. **Medicare taxes**
   Multiply line 1 by 2.9 % (0.029)
4. **Federal income taxes withheld**
5. **Add lines 2,3, and 4**

   ☐ If cash wages no more than $1,000 in ANY calendar
   QUARTER, enter line 5 on Form 1040.

   ☐ **Otherwise** continue through Part II.

Part II	Federal Unemployment (FUTA) Tax

State Unemployment Contributions: ☐ Yes ; ☐ No

Subpart A

6. **Contributions to State unemployment fund**
7. **Cash wages subject to FUTA tax**
8. **FUTA tax.** Multiply line 7 by 0.8% (0.008)

Subpart B

Complex 10 columns of "State Experience" Computations

9. Contributions due & payable to State
10. FUTA tax. Multiply line 7 by 6.2% (0.062)
11. State UI tax. Multiply line 7 by 5.4% (0.054)
12. Enter **smaller of** line 9 or line 11
13. FUTA tax. Subtract line 12 from line 10
14. Add lines 5, 8, OR 13. Enter on Form 1040

Fig. 6.1 - Simplified Arrangement of Parts I and II of Schedule H (1040)

summary of Parts I and II. If Part II is not required, Part III is not required either.

The biggest hassle of Schedule H is its Part II: the FUTA tax. After you have answered three Yes-No questions, Part II boils down to two subparts: A and B. Subpart A says that, if you paid your State unemployment agency all that it demands of you, the FUTA tax rate is a mere 0.8% (0.008). Subpart B applies when you have not responded to all state agency demands. In this case, the FUTA tax rate is 6.2% (0.062). By comparison, the Social Security tax that you pay on your domestic workers is 12.4% (0.124). The Medicare tax rate is 2.9% (0.029). Altogether, the grand total employment tax rate is 21.5% (0.062 + 0.124 + 0.029). For example, if you paid a particular worker $5,295 for the year, your total employment tax would be $1,138 (5,295 x 0.215). This amount comes exclusively out of your pocket. The employee pays none of it. You are providing him/her some degree of security.

There's More than Schedule H

If Schedule H were all that you had to do once a year, the aggravation would not be too bad. Particularly so, if you could avoid its Part II by paying out total cash wages of $1,000 or less for any calendar quarter. Unfortunately, Schedule H alone is not all there is to it.

First off, before you can even attach Schedule H to your Form 1040, you have to get from the IRS an *Employer Identification Number* (EIN). This means preparing separately an 18-line **Form SS-4**: Application for EIN. Three pages of instructions accompany this form. Yes, you can apply for an EIN by phone, but before doing so, you have to have a filled-out SS-4 form by your side. After being assigned an EIN (9 digits), you enter this number *below* your SSN at the top of Schedule H.

Since *you* now have one or more employees and you pay them wages, you have to become familiar with Forms **W-2**, **W-3**, **W-4**, and **W-5**. Realistically, you could eliminate Form W-4: Employee's Withholding Allowance Certificate, and Form W-5: Earned Income Credit Advance Payment Certificate. But you cannot eliminate Forms W-2 and W-3.

Form W-2: *Wage and Tax Statement* is already familiar to you. Your employer filled it out for you. The difference now is that *you* have to fill out one set of W-2s for each of your household workers. A "set" of W-2s consists of six copies: A, B, 1, 2, C, and D. There are eight pages of instructions to tell you how to complete each set. Copy A goes to the Social Security Administration; copy B is attached by the employee to his/her Federal tax return; copy 1 goes to the taxing agency of your state of domicile; copy 2 is attached by the employee to his/her state return; copy C is for your employee's records; and copy D is for your records.

There is — finally — Form W-3: *Transmittal of Wage and Tax Statements.* This is a summary of all wages paid, all social security/medicare taxes paid, and all income tax withheld, if any, for the calendar year just ended. Copy A of each W-2 attaches to the primary copy of Form W-3, which is submitted en masse to the Social Security Administration. The "where to file" the W-3 is given in its accompanying three pages of instruction. Keep the copy marked "YOUR COPY" for your files.

All of the above assumes that you are able to minimize any undue hassle with State taxing agencies. If you live in an aggressive unemployment/disability insurance taxing state, read on. You may want to change your tactics about this whole nanny tax affair.

California Goes Bonkers

California considers itself the 5th sovereign nation of the world. Based on its GDP (gross domestic product), it probably is. As a result, it disregards the IRS's Schedule H and imposes its own employment tax burdens and thresholds.

The California employment tax menu consists of:

(1)   Unemployment insurance tax (UI) @ 3.4%
(2)   Employment training tax (ETT)   @ 0.1%
(3)   State disability insurance tax (SDI) @ <u>0.5%</u>
                                  Total   4.0%

These taxes are payable quarterly or annually, depending on the total *household* wages that you pay to your workers during the year. Incidentally, the term "household wages" is the sum of cash wages PLUS *all noncash benefits* in the form of food, clothing, shelter, entertainment, transportation, gifts, etc. This noncash element adds a whole new dimension to employee wage recordkeeping.

To start the California process, you file Form DE lHW: *Registration Form for Employers of Household Workers*. This form is required the moment you first pay $750 and 1 cent in cash wages during a calendar quarter. Your "registration" is the assignment of an 8-digit Account Number (e.g. 123-4567-8) by the Employment Development Department (EDD), State of California. This locks you into an **8-year** EDD surveillance program. Throughout this 8-year period, irrespective of wages paid, you must report to EDD the name, address, social security number, and start-of-work date for each and every domestic worker you hire. Use Form DE 34: *Report of New Employee(s)* to do so. Upon being EDD registered, you are sent a **64-page** book of instructions relating to forms, payment dates, and tax rates.

You are also sent Form DE 98: *Employer of Household Worker Election*. This form allows you to elect an annual payment plan, IF you intend to pay no more than $20,000 in "subject wages." If you so elect, you still have to make FOUR quarterly reports each on Form DE 3B HW: *Quarterly Report of Wages and Withholdings for Employers of Household Workers*. Note that these quarterlies are "reports": not returns. No payments are attached. Your annual payment is made on Form DE 3HW: *Annual Payroll Tax Return for Employer of Household Workers*.

Rethink Your Household Needs

If you reside in a state that takes a hard line and adversarial stance on employment tax issues, maybe you should rethink your intentions about having household employees. Maybe you don't need such persons as much as you think. Or, maybe you don't need them at all. Much depends on the age(s) and number of dependents that you have to provide care for. Much also depends on your repertoire of family members, neighbors, and friends that you can call upon — and pay — for nonofficial assistance. Must all your dependents' care needs be provided in your home, or can some or all be provided outside of your home?

Strictly as a guide for your rethinking purposes, we present in Figure 6.2 our formulation of four categories of dependents that you

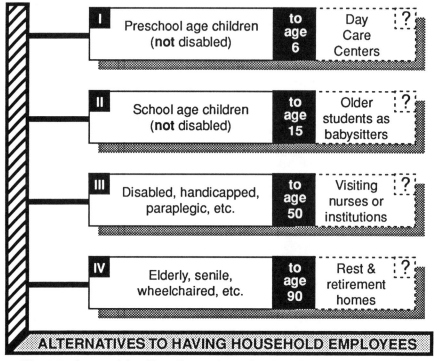

Fig. 6.2 - Categorizing Your Dependents for Care Providing Decisions

may have. We categorize I and II as your "most likely" range of dependents. Categories III and IV are "also likely" dependents, but probably fewer in number than categories I (preschool-age children) and II (school-age children). We limit categories I and II to normal children without handicaps or special needs.

If you have preschool-age children (up to age 6 or so), the existence of registered day-care centers is a growing industry of its own. For two working parents with preschoolers, taking them to day-care centers in the morning and picking them up in the afternoon is a common trend. Some corporate employers sponsor or provide their own day-care centers on their own premises. Others allow flex hours to parents with young children. Under these circumstances, we see no need for your becoming a household employer, which requires your registering with your state.

In those areas where day-care centers are simply not available, you still need to think through the necessity for engaging a nanny in your home. Try the best that you can to get an out-care nanny service, where you take the child to the care provider. If it turns out that in-home nanny care is your only recourse, weigh seriously your limited tax benefits against the aggravation of employment tax liabilities to your state of domicile. If your and your spouse's incomes combined are high enough, could you afford to absorb the nanny cost on your own, without claiming any tax benefits? In most two wage-earner cases with gross incomes over $100,000, because of phaseout rules, the benefits are negligible. Why expose yourself to the reporting and tax aggravation of being a household employer?

In the case of school-age children (category II in Figure 6.2), we do not see the need for your ever being a household employer. Surely, somewhere in your family (your parents, nieces, nephews, etc.), among your neighbors, or in your circle of friends, there is someone who would accept pin money for now-and-then babysitting tasks. If this approach is unsuccessful, try advertising in high school and junior college media for the temporary help that you need. Most students are cavalier about any tax obligations they might have. After all, they are students. At least under Federal law — and some states, too — students are exempt from employment tax reportings and payments. The *character* of the students you employ is very important. Screen them critically for their use of drugs, booze, pornography, and Internet wagering. You want conscientious students who are good examples for your children.

The Disabled & Elderly

Providing for the care and well-being of disabled dependents (Category III in Figure 6.2) is heart wrenching and difficult. We define disabled dependents as those of any age (typically, 5 to 50) who have had serious medical problems in their lives: birth defects (Down's syndrome), rare diseases (encephalitis), freak accidents (bullet in head from July 4th celebration), and mysterious onsets (spinal meningitis, multiple sclerosis). These are case-by-case situations. In addition to TLC (tender loving care) from family members, trained and experienced health-aide-type caretakers are needed. High-school and college students will not do.

Depending on the nature of the disability or handicap, two approaches could be considered. If only occasional or part-time supervision is needed, explore a "visiting nurse" arrangement with a hospital or physician's service. If special diet or food needs are to be prepared, engage a "meals on wheels" type service. Otherwise, if full care is needed, explore out-of-home special needs providers or private institutions.

Unfortunately, out-of-home services for disabled persons tend to be expensive, tend to go on for years, and tend to be impersonal. For these reasons, it may be more prudent for one of the spousal taxpayers to forego or rearrange his/her employment activities (e.g., working at home is in vogue these days).

In the case of having elderly dependents (the extreme elderly, senile, wheelchaired, bedridden, or otherwise infirm), placement in a rest or retirement home is common practice these days. Unfortunately, sometimes, mistreatment of the elderly can occur. If the elderly person (usually your parent, your spouse's parent, or a sibling of your parent) is competent mentally, the role of in-home "independent contractors" could be explored.

Independent Contractors: Yes; No

An *independent contractor* is a person who is "in business for himself/herself." He/she is not an employee of someone, nor is someone his/her employer. The individual is SELF EMPLOYED.

Independent contractors are persons preferably over the age of 35, who are *tax mature*, who work for more than one principal at a time, and who are self-motivated to do the best job they can. They are not seeking now-and-then activities for pin money, nor are they seeking money-under-the-table to avoid its taxation. These are persons who hold themselves out as professionals in household care. Often, they are licensed, registered, or certified in some manner. These and other qualities that we list in Figure 6.3 are essential, if that person's independent status is to be upheld.

The IRS and state employment tax agencies are paranoid about independent contractors. Tax agents view such persons as schemers trying to avoid the payment of social security, medicare, income, unemployment, and disability insurance taxes. If you contract with

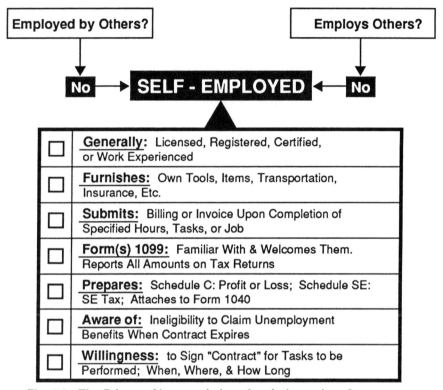

Fig. 6.3 - The Primary Characteristics of an Independent Contractor

these persons to do household tasks, you are deemed to be a co-conspirator in a bizarre scheme to avoid your paying all employment taxes. Upon reaching this closed-mind "determination," tax agencies will reclassify as employees all independent contractors that you have ever had. The agency goal is to max tax you, penalize you, and tax brutalize you . . . to "teach you a lesson."

Nevertheless, stick to what is right and stick to your convictions. After all, the work is performed in your own private home. Don't you have the right to engage employees or nonemployees as you see fit? Employment tax agencies insist that you do **not** have such right. What do you do?

First, you solicit simultaneously two or three qualified independent contractors who provide home-care services. The hallmark of such persons is their independence to work for two, three, five, or more principals during the same monthly time frame. You want them on staggered different days to meet your dependent's changing needs.

Second, when interviewing them, ask point blank about their filing income tax returns. Ask them specifically about their Schedules C (Form 1040): *Profit or Loss from Business.* Ask about their Schedules SE (Form 1040): *Self-Employment Tax.* Ask about their familiarity with Forms 1099-MISC: *Miscellaneous Income*; Box 7: *Nonemployee compensation.* Ask to see the latest three years of their returns. You are not to probe their personal affairs. You want to be assured that they are TAX MATURE, and not using you as a scapegoat for their taxes.

Third, write up a simple contract for each contractor and you to sign. State that you will issue a 1099-MISC at the end of the calendar year, and that each contractor will file his/her own Schedule C and Schedule SE, as required. Make it clear that the remuneration you pay is not wages; it is compensation for contracted services, the itemization of which you both agree to. Also make it clear that the contractor is not eligible for Federal or State unemployment compensation when the terms of the contract expire. Have the contractors confirm their knowledge that as self-employed persons they are automatically ineligible for unemployment benefits. Applying for such benefits contradicts the tenets of being an independent contractor. Specify their billing or invoicing procedure to you, then have the "contract" witnessed or notarized.

If independent contractors can fulfill the household-care tasks that your dependent(s) need, your year-end tax paperwork duties are greatly simplified. For each contractor, you prepare one Form 1099-MISC. You attach all said 1099s to Form 1096: *Annual Summary and Transmittal of U.S. Information Returns.* Indicate the number of 1099s attached, grand total the amount you paid for the year, then mail the whole works to the IRS Service Center directed on the form. Send nothing to a state employment tax agency. No Schedule H (Form 1040) is necessary, either.

7

EDUCATION TAX CREDITS

> There Are Two Independent Education Credits: HOPE Scholarship And LIFETIME Learning. The Maximum Hope Credit Is $1,500 "Per Student." No One Student Is Eligible For More Than Two Years. The Maximum Lifetime Credit Is $2,000 "Per Taxpayer." There Is No Limit To The Number Of Years This Credit May Be Claimed. Each Credit Is Based On The Amount Of "Qualified Tuition And Related Expenses" That Are REQUIRED TO BE PAID To An Accredited Institution For Enrollment. Whereas The Hope Credit Focuses On Acquiring A Degree By Certificate, The Lifetime Credit Focuses On Acquiring Or Improving Job Skills.

Note the plural "s" — credits — in the chapter heading. This is to alert you to the fact that *two* separate educational tax credits can be claimed. One is called the *Hope Scholarship Credit* and the other is called the *Lifetime Learning Credit*. These are nonrefundable credits with no exclusion counterpart. They are allowable only if — after subtracting certain other credits — there is any residual tax after computing your tentative tax (regular tax plus alternative minimum tax). For the "pecking order" of the nonrefundable credits, recall Figure 4.3 on page 4-9.

The Form 1040 (page 2) on which you can claim the Hope and Lifetime credits lists them as—

Education credits. Attach Form 8863.

What this clearly implies is that both credits can be claimed on the same tax form. A bold printed *Caution* on the form says—

You cannot take the hope credit and the lifetime learning credit for the same student.

However, in the same family, one student can claim the hope credit while another student claims the lifetime credit. The hope credit is limited to the first two years of post-secondary education, whereas the lifetime credit is not limited in the number of years that can be claimed. Hence, the term: *lifetime learning*.

Both credits (under different subsections) are prescribed in IRC Section 25A: *Hope and Lifetime Learning Credits*. We are not sure as to the origin of the term "Hope" but we suspect that it has something to do with "hoping to go to college." In subsection 25A(b), it is designated as a "scholarship" credit. Both credits phase out entirely when the parents' adjusted gross income exceeds $100,000 (more specifically, $102,000 for year 2002).

In this chapter, obviously, we want to introduce you to the features of Section 25A and its many ramifications. We particularly want to explain what is meant by: (1) eligible student; (2) eligible education institution; (3) qualified tuition expenses; (4) payments by third parties (such as by grandparents, uncles, aunts); (5) credit base and limitations, and (6) the "attachment" of Form 8813. The whole idea behind Section 25A is to motivate low- and middle-income parents with high-school-age children on their hands to direct them towards college and higher education levels. Though the dollar amounts of the credits allowed do not cover all of the tuition and fees involved, the credits do go a long way towards reducing parents' actual out-of-pocket costs.

Overview of Section 25A

As already mentioned, the title of Section 25A is: *Hope and Lifetime Learning Credits*. The one tax law alone comprises more than 2,000 words, and is accompanied by more than 8,000 regulatory words (*well over* 10,000 total). With this amount of tax wording, you should expect restrictive conditions and qualifications to apply. And they do. Neither credit is intended to be claimed unless there is good justification in the educational arena for it.

The general purpose of Section 25A is its subsection (a): *Allowance of Credit.* This approximately 40-word subsection says—

> *In the case of an **individual**, there shall be allowed as a credit against the tax imposed . . . for the taxable year the amount equal to the sum of—*
>
> *(1) the Hope Scholarship Credit, plus*
> *(2) the Lifetime Learning Credit.*

Note our emphasis on the term: *individual.* Such a person may be a single parent, two parents (filing jointly), a grandparent (perhaps), a student, or other dependent. Educational payments made by corporations, partnerships, proprietorships, limited liability companies, and trusts that are owned by parents of students simply do not qualify for the credit. Only those direct out-of-pocket expenditures paid or incurred for higher education by individuals count towards the credit allowable. You'll receive evidence of this on Form 1098-T: *Tuition Payments Statement.*

There is much more to Section 25A than its subsection (a) above. The best way to overview its other eight subsections — (b) through (i) — is to list them for you in Figure 7.1. Included in our listing are the paragraphs and subparagraphs which carry their own subheadings, within each subsection. We think it will be instructive for you to take a moment now to skim down the listing of titles, subtitles, and captions displayed in Figure 7.1.

We'll cover the important highlights of Figure 7.1 as we go along. Meanwhile, we want to call your immediate attention to subsections (**b**)(**1**) and (**c**)(**1**). Their respective titles are:

Subsec. (b) — Hope Scholarship Credit
Para. (1) — *Per student credit*

Subsec. (c) — Lifetime Learning Credit
Para. (1) — *Per taxpayer credit*

FAMILY TAX STRATEGIES

Section 25A	HOPE AND LIFETIME LEARNING [TAX] CREDITS	

Subsection	Para.	Sub. Para.	Title, Subtitle, or Caption
(b)			Hope Scholarship Credit
	(1)		Per Student Credit
	(2)		Limitations Applicable To Hope Credit
		(A)	Credit Only For Two Taxable Years
		(B)	Credit Only If At Least 1/2 Time Student
		(C)	Credit Only For First 2 Years Of Postsecondary Ed
		(D)	No Credit If Convicted Of Felony Drug Offense
	(3)		Eligible Student
	(4)		Applicable Limit
(c)			Lifetime Learning Credit
	(1)		Per Taxpayer Credit
	(2)		Rules For Determining Expenses
		(A)	Coordination With Hope Credit
		(B)	Expenses Eligible For Credit
(d)			Limitation Based On Modified Adjusted Gross Income
	(1)		In General
	(2)		Amount Of Reduction
	(3)		Modified Adjusted Gross Income
(e)			Election Not To Have Section Apply
(f)			Definitions
	(1)		Qualified Tuition And Related Expenses
		(A)	General Meaning Of Term
		(B)	Exceptions For Eduction Involving Sports, Etc.
		(C)	Exception For Nonacademic Fees
	(2)		Eligible Educational Institution
(g)			Special Rules
	(1)		Identification Requirement
	(2)		Adjustment For Certain Scholarships, Etc.
	(3)		Treatment Of Expenses Paid By Dependent
	(4)		Treatment Of Certain Prepayments
	(5)		Denial If Double Benefit
	(6)		No Credit For Married Filing Separate Returns
	(7)		Nonresident Aliens
(h)			Inflation Adjustments
(i)			Regulations

Fig. 7.1 - Listing of Titles and Captions in IRC Section 25A

7-4

"Per student"; "Per taxpayer": What's the difference?

The maximum per student Hope credit is $1,500 for each of no more than two years. This means that if parents were supporting three students in college simultaneously, they could, under the proper conditions, claim a $4,500 credit for each of two years. Thereafter, the Hope credit would cease altogether.

The maximum per taxpayer Lifetime credit is $2,000 per year regardless of the number of students a taxpayer supports. However, the $2,000 credit can be claimed *each year* over a lifetime of eligible learning. There is simply no two-year limitation, as in the case of the per-student limitation. Over a period of 10 eligible years, for example, you could claim as much as $20,000 in cumulative lifetime learning credits.

Hope Credit Specifics

Let's expand on subsection (b)(1) re the Hope credit. Its principal wording is its paragraph (1): ***Per student credit.*** This paragraph reads—

*In the case of an eligible student **for whom an election is in effect** . . . for any taxable year, the Hope Scholarship Credit is . . . the sum of—*

    *(A)   100 percent of so much of the qualified tuition and related expenses paid . . . during the taxable year (for education furnished . . . during any academic period beginning in such taxable year) as does not exceed $1,000, **plus***

    (B)   50 percent of such expenses so paid as exceeds $1,000 but does not exceed [$500].

Add subparagraphs (A) and (B) together and you come up with $1,500 as the maximum Hope credit allowable. Inflation adjustments in $100 increments are allowed in excess of the $1,500.

Particularly note in the citation above the emphasized phrase: *for whom an election is in effect.* What is this all about? You'll be able to focus better on the answer once you realize that the Hope credit is a "scholarship" form of credit.

Ordinarily, financial assistance in the form of scholarship awards is not taxable income. Student financial assistance is often offered by employers, veterans affairs, educational institutions, and charitable trusts. Since this award money is not taxable, it does not qualify for a tax credit when used to pay tuition and fees to an educational institution. Only that money which is taxable to the recipient qualifies for the credit claim. This is a tax principle of long standing. Nontaxable money has already enjoyed a tax benefit; its use does not give rise to another tax benefit.

The idea of an "election" simply means that the credit claimant agrees not to use the awards money for any otherwise eligible credit-claiming expenditures. There is no prohibition against using both taxable and nontaxable money, so long as the expenditures from each class are separate and distinct from one another. This is purely a documentation and recordkeeping matter.

The election is exercised by timely filing an income tax return (including extensions) with Form 8863: *Education Credits*, attached to it. Since this form includes claims for both the Hope and Lifetime credits, the election requirement applies also to the Lifetime Learning credit.

Lifetime Credit Specifics

The statutory wording of subsection (c)(1): *Per taxpayer credit*, reads primarily as—

The Lifetime Learning Credit for any taxpayer for any taxable year is an amount equal to 20 percent of so much of the qualified tuition and related expenses paid . . . (for education furnished during any academic period beginning in such taxable year) as does not exceed $10,000.

The 20% of $10,000 is $2,000. Said amount is the maximum credit allowable to any one taxpayer in any one taxable year. The $10,000 expense base can be adjusted for inflation in $1,000 increments. This means an additional $200 credit per year, depending on the official rate of inflation.

Closely associated with the above is paragraph (2)(A) of subsection (c): *Coordination with Hope Scholarship*. The idea here is that any educational expense claimed under the Hope credit . . . *shall not be taken into account* (for the Lifetime credit). This is an old-old tax principle. If you claim a tax credit or deduction for one set of expenditures, using the same set of expenditures you cannot turn around and claim another credit or deduction.

There is also another aspect of the "coordination" concept of subsection (c)(1)(A). Because the Hope and Lifetime credits are so similar in purpose, the Hope credit becomes your reference base for nearly all of the qualifying conditions for claiming either credit. For example, the term: *qualified tuition and related expenses* is used identically for both credits. Other terms are, too. We think of the coordination aspect as a hand-and-glove affair between the two credits. We depict this aspect for you in Figure 7.2.

On the other hand, the term: *eligible student*, stands out in the Hope credit, but is silent in the Lifetime credit. In its place, the term: *any taxpayer*, is used. This is recognition of the fact that the educational goals are different between a student and a taxpayer. Generally, a student is not considered a working taxpayer, whereas a taxpayer is not considered an ordinary student. Age is not a factor for either credit.

Eligible Student Defined

Of the two educational credits, the Hope credit is the more dominant in terms of statutory definitions. In this respect, Regulation § 1.25A-3(d)(1): *Eligible student defined*, requires that such a person be—

(i)   enrolled in an *eligible education institution* recognized by the U.S. Department of Education under the Higher Education Act of 1965. Such an institution is any accredited public, private, or nonprofit college, university, vocational school, or postsecondary educational facility.

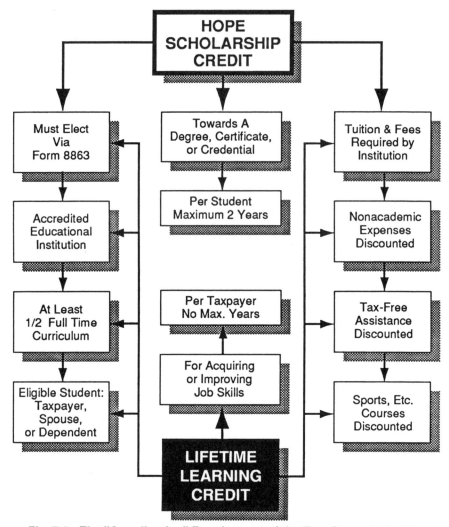

Fig. 7.2 - The "Coordination" Requirement of the Two Separate Credits

(ii)   enrolled for at least one academic period that begins during the taxable year, in a program that leads to a postsecondary degree, *certificate, or credential*;

(iii)   enrolled for *at least half of the normal full-time work load* for the course of study being pursued;

(iv) as of the *beginning* of the taxable year, *not have completed the first two years* of postsecondary education (disregarding any academic credits awarded strictly on proficiency exams without attending class); and

(v) *without* any federal or state *felony convictions* for the *possession or distribution of a controlled substance* as of the end of the taxable year for which the credit is claimed.

An "academic period" is that length of time (quarter, semester, summer) which is established by the institution as qualifying for its academic credits. The term "postsecondary" means post high school: the freshman and sophomore years of college. The objective in these first two years of college must be some form of recognized degree, certificate, or credential. The idea is to qualify the participating student for a higher-than-high-school occupational livelihood, should he/she not complete a full curriculum at college.

The Hope credit is based strictly on a degree course of study. In contrast, the Lifetime credit recognizes either a degree course or a nondegree course, or a combination of both. The "lifetime learning" idea is to encourage aspirants to acquire or improve job skills, irrespective of whether they wind up with an academic degree or not. In all other respects, the student eligibility requirements are the same for both credits.

Qualified Tuition & Fees

The allowability of either credit is contingent upon the educational expenditures being: *qualified tuition and related expenses*. Furthermore, the qualified expenses are only those which are **paid directly to** the educational institution itself. The payment is a condition of the student's enrollment or attendance at the institution. In other words, the amount paid must be a **required fee**.

Regulation § 1.25A-2(d): *Definition*, points out clearly that qualified expenses—

Include fees for books, supplies, and equipment used in a course of study . . . and other nonacademic fees . . . only if paid to the *eligible institution for the enrollment or attendance of the student. Qualified expenses **do not include** the costs of room and board, insurance, medical expenses, transportation, and similar personal, living, or family expenses, regardless of whether or not paid to the institution for the enrollment or attendance.* [Emphasis added.]

If a student is required to pay a comprehensive fee that includes tuition, fees, and personal expenses, the portion allocable to personal expenses is not a qualified tuition and related expense. Nor do qualified expenses include any course of instruction that involves sports, games, hobbies, or other noncredit endeavor. This is the "hobby course" rule. Exceptions apply where such course is an integral part of the (Hope) student's degree program, or part of the (Lifetime) student's effort to acquire or improve job skills.

In way of summary at this point, we present in Figure 7.3 the key features of what constitutes qualified tuition and fees. As always (and we've mentioned this earlier), the use of any tax-free educational assistance to defray the required enrollment expenses does not qualify. As always, also, good documentation is required to support the expenses claimed for each student for each type of tax credit claimed.

Other Related Rules

There are numerous other matters related to a student's qualifying expenses for the Hope and Lifetime tax credits. Foremost in this regard is what we call the "for whom" rule. That is, for whom are the tuition and fees paid? The answer lies in subsection (f)(1): *Definitions; Qualified . . . Expenses.* Said expenses are—

tuition and fees required for the enrollment or attendance of—

   (i)   the taxpayer,

   (ii)   the taxpayer's spouse, or

   (iii)   any dependent of the taxpayer

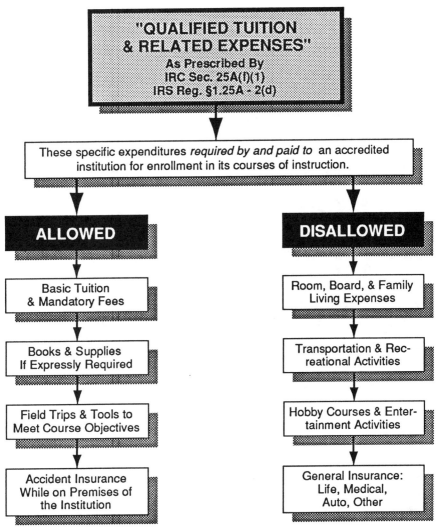

Fig. 7.3 - Summary of "Qualified Expenses" For Education Tax Credits

. . . at an eligible institution for courses of instruction of such individual.

There is also the "prepayment" rule: subsection (g)(4): **Certain Prepayments.** The essence here is that, if the qualified tuition and fees are prepaid for an academic period—

which begins during the first 3 months following the taxable year [of the prepayment], *such academic period shall be treated . . . as beginning during* [the prepayment] *taxable year.*

When qualified expenses are paid by a student who is claimed by a parent as a dependent, the parent may claim the tax credit. This follows from the general rule that dependents are not required to pay from their own funds for their own support and education.

On the other hand, if a grandparent makes the qualified payments, the parent (if the student is a dependent of the parent) may claim the credit The payment is treated as a gift from the grandparent to the parent, who in turn pays the institution. But, if the student is not a dependent of the parent, the grandparent's payment is treated as paid by the student, thereby enabling the student to claim the tax credit.

No Hope or Lifetime credits are allowed to married individuals who file separate returns. This is so regardless of which parent claims the student as a dependent. If a parent or student is a nonresident alien, neither of the two credits is applicable. However, a nonresident alien always has the option of electing to be a resident alien by filing a U.S. tax return in order to claim either credit.

Form 8863, Parts I and II

To claim one or both of the Section 25A credits, the use of **Form 8863** is required. This form is titled: ***Education Credits (Hope and Lifetime Learning Credits)***. We would have preferred this title to be: Education *Tax* Credits, so as to avoid any misconception of being associated with academic credits. Part I of Form 8863 computes the Hope Scholarship credit for *each* student listed thereon. Part II computes the *aggregate* Lifetime Learning credit for different students listed thereon. Part I is a "per student credit" times the number of students listed. Part II is a "per taxpayer credit" which combines all students for one total maximum credit. An abridged version of these two parts of Form 8863 is presented in Figure 7.4. Note that we also show a Part III , but refer you to subsequent text.

Form 8863	EDUCATION [TAX] CREDITS • See Instructions • Attach to Form 1040	Year

Your Name: _____ Your SSN: _____

Part I Hope Scholarship Credit

(a) Student's Name	(b) Student's SSN	(c) Expenses up to $2,000	(d) Smaller of (c) or $1,000	(e) Subtract (d) from (c)	(f) One-half of col. (e)

ADD amounts in (d); also (f) ⟶ ▨▨▨▨

Tentative credit: ADD columns (d) and (f) ⟶ ☐

Part II Lifetime Learning Credit

Student's Name	Student's SSN	Qualified Expenses

ADD all amounts in "qualified expense" column ⟶

Enter SMALLER of above or $10,000 ----------▶

Tentative credit: Multiply smaller amout by 20% ⟶ ☐

Part III Allowable Education Credits

ADD tentative credits, Parts I and II . . . . ⟶	1.
PHASE OUT COMPUTATIONS • See Text • See Instructions	2. ▨▨▨ 3. 4. 5.
	6.
Potential tentative amount . . . . ⟶	7.
Enter regular tax plus AMT	8.
Enter total of three priority credits	9.
SUBTRACT step 9 from step 8	10.
Education credits: Enter SMALLER of step 7 or step 10 ▶	11.

Fig. 7.4 - Abridged Version of Form 8863 for Claiming Education Credits

As mentioned earlier, you cannot claim both credits for the *same* student. You can claim one credit or the other. But if, as a parent, you have two children who are college bound, one student can qualify for the Hope credit, while the other student qualifies for the Lifetime credit. You can also treat yourself and your spouse as two separate students. Let us illustrate, by assuming that you have four dependent children.

Suppose, for example, you list in Part I three of your children as eligible students. Form 8863 has preprinted lines and columns for three students . . . *whose SSN's are also shown on page 1 of your tax return.* You fill in the columnar spaces and compute your credits for each student to be $1,200; $1,300; and $1,500, respectively. At this point, your Part I *tentative* credit is $4,000 (1,200 + 1,400 + 1,500). Recall from earlier comments that the maximum separate credit per student is $1,500.

In Part II, you also have three students listed: yourself, your spouse, and one child different from those in Part I. The qualifying expenses, respectively, are: $4,500; $3,500; and $5,000. Instructions on Form 8863 tell you to add the three amounts, then enter the **smaller** of the total or $10,000. When added, the total is $13,000 (4,500 + 3,500 + 5,000). Obviously, $10,000 is smaller than $13,000. The *tentative* allowable credit is 20% of $10,000 . . . which is $2,000.

Using the illustrative numbers above, the two tentative tax credits are:

Part I   —   Hope Scholarship $4,000 for 3 students
Part II —   Lifetime Learning $2,000 for 3 different students

Obviously, if you had a choice, and a student were otherwise eligible, you'd prefer listing that student in Part I. But you can only do so for no more than two years for the same student. While Part II provides a lower per student credit, there is no limit to the number of years that the Part II credit can be claimed. You can claim the same student for multiple years, or multiple students over multiple years.

Part III: The Credit Phaseout

The tax credits established in Parts I and II of Form 8863 are tentative only. We stressed this point by italicizing the word "tentative" in two places above: re Part I and, separately, re Part II. In Part III, the two credits are combined, then are subjected to a phase-out computation. Part III is titled: *Allowable Education Credits.* After the phaseout subtraction, if any, the bottom line of Form 8863 is one credit amount which is "allowable," At this point, there is no distinction between the Part I and the Part II credits. When combined, they are: *Education credits.* They enter as one amount on one line on page 2 of Form 1040.

The phaseout process is set forth in Section 25A(d): *Limitation Based on Modified Adjusted Gross Income* (AGI). The actual statutory wording is too awkward and confusing to cite here. Part III of Form 8863 steps you through the limitation computations in a rather complex way. We urge that you get an official Form 8863 and skim read the preprinted instructions in Part III thereof. Then, after reviewing the below, reread the instructions one line at a time. There are 11 such lines. Four of these lines refer to certain line numbers on Form 1040 and, separately, to other line numbers on Form 1040A. This, too often, can cause errors. Your *modified* AGI is your regular AGI **increased** by any exclusion of income from foreign sources, Puerto Rico, and American Samoa (a U.S. possession).

The essence of Part III is that, if your modified AGI exceeds $100,000 (married filing jointly) or $50,000 (all others except married filing separately), **none** of the Section 25A tax credits are allowable. They "phase out" completely. This means that you have to look to other sections of the tax code for education tax benefits. We cover the "other sections" quite extensively in Chapter 8 (coming up). Meanwhile, Section 25A(g)(6) makes it clear that no credits are allowed to *married persons filing separate returns.*

If your modified AGI is $80,000 or less (married joint) or $40,000 or less (others except married separate), the tentative credits in Parts I and II are allowed in full. It is between $80,000 and $100,000 married joint (and between $40,000 and $50,000 for others except married separate) that the phaseout rule applies.

In the simplest terms possible, the phaseouts go like this:

Married Joint:
$$\frac{100,000 - \text{Modified AGI}}{\$20,000} \times \text{tentative credit} = \$_____$$

Others Except M/S:
$$\frac{50,000 - \text{Modified AGI}}{\$10,000} \times \text{tentative credit} = \$_____$$

To make matters a bit more complicated, the $100,000/$50,000 amounts are indexed each year for inflation.

Form 8863: Bottom Line

It takes eleven official lines/steps in Part III to arrive at a combined tentative education tax credit. We indicated these eleven steps in Figure 7.4. For illustration purposes, let us assume that the entry amount at step 7 (tentative amount) is $6,000. There are four more steps to go: 8 through 11. At step 8, you enter your regular tax plus AMT (alternative minimum tax). Suppose you entered $5,000. At step 9, you add and enter any foreign tax credit, dependent care credit, and elderly/disabled credit that you may have claimed. Suppose you entered $600 at step 9. At step 10, you are instructed to subtract step 9 ($600) from step 8 ($5,000), leaving $4,400 (5,000 – 600) for entry thereon.

Step 11 is the very bottom line of Form 8863. The preprinted instruction there says—

> *Education credits. Enter the smaller of* [step 7 or step 10] *here, and on* [page 2] *of Form 1040.*

Inserting the illustrative dollar amounts above, step 7 is $6,000 and step 10 is $4,400. The "smaller of" is obviously $4,400. Here's a situation where your tentatively allowable credit is $6,000 but your officially allowable amount is $4,400 — a difference of $1,600. What happens to this $1,600 unallowable credit?

Answer: You lose it entirely. It is nonrefundable. This is because you wiped out all tax showing at step 8. You get no credit carryover like the child adoption credit in Chapter 5.

8

OTHER EDUCATION INCENTIVES

There Are NINE Tax Code Sections Which Create Incentives For You to Contine Your Education, And For Your Spouse And Your Dependents To Continue Theirs. The Gamut Includes Limited Exclusions From Gross Income, Adjustments To Gross Income, Miscellaneous Itemized Deductions, And Earnings On After-Tax Plans. All Expenditures Must Be For TUITION, FEES, BOOKS, And SUPPLIES Required By An "Eligible" Educational Institution. In Certain Cases, Expenditures May Include ROOM And BOARD, And SPECIAL NEEDS SERVICES For Handicapped Students. There Is Some AGI Means Testing; Any "Excess Benefits" Are Taxable.

As previous chapters have shown, there are certain tax benefits (credits, mostly) to the family unit when there are children and dependents. It is only natural, therefore, that there be certain tax incentives to encourage higher education among other family members. For such incentives, the term "higher education" means higher than one's current educational level, whatever that level may be: primary, secondary, undergraduate, or graduate.

In general terms, there are four stages of higher educational incentives with respect to Form 1040. There are (1) the exclusion stage, (2) the adjustment stage, (3) the deduction stage, and (4) the exemption-after-tax stage.

An "exclusion" means that the allowable amount is excluded from gross income. It is not shown, nor is it required to be shown, in the income portion (page 1) of Form 1040. An "adjustment" is a subtraction from total income that appears near the bottom portion of page 1. The subsequent result is your Adjusted Gross Income (AGI). A "deduction" is an expenditure — an expense — that appears on Schedule A: *Itemized Deductions*, Schedule C: *Profit or Loss from Business*, and Schedule E: *Supplemental Income and Loss*, which attach to Form 1040. An "exemption after tax" means that after-tax money has been used to set up a qualified savings plan for educational purposes. While *in the plan*, the earnings on the after-tax money are exempt from tax. Long-term savings plans benefit substantially from this exemption feature.

Altogether, there is a total of nine tax incentives (in **addition** to the HOPE and LIFETIME credits in Chapter 7) for acquiring, enhancing, and continuing one's educational goals. Each of the nine separate benefits is prescribed by a particular Internal Revenue Code section (and its regulations). As with all tax benefits, the educational incentives are not unlimited. In each case, the principal limitation is your income level — AGI — which often causes the benefits to phase out in their entirety. There are different AGI thresholds, depending on the type of benefit sought. As you'll see shortly, not all benefits are AGI-sensitive.

Meanwhile, in this chapter we want to review in a meaningful way all nine of the higher and continuing educational tax incentives. By this, we want you to know where they appear, or do not appear, on your tax return, to what extent they apply, and what value they may be in your overall tax planning endeavors. As is always the case, no one group of tax benefits or incentives can eliminate all income tax. But, if fully used where applicable, they can be very helpful in reducing such tax.

In all, there are 11 (9+Hope+Lifetime) education tax incentives available to every family with one or more eligible students. If you "max out" one option, one or more other options might apply. So long as you do not claim the same expenditure twice, theoretically all 11 options could be used in the same taxable year.

There is one particularly attractive feature about tax incentives towards higher education. They are not limited strictly to children and dependents who are part- or full-time students. Some incentives apply to occupationally active adults who are seeking to improve themselves financially. The rationale of Congress seems to be that the more education you acquire, the more money you make, the more tax you pay.

List of the 9 Incentives

The nine educational tax incentives are scattered throughout the Internal Revenue Code in no logical order. In pure numerical sequencing, they start at Section 72 and extend through Section 530. This gamut spans over 450 tax code sections, of which only nine are pertinent to our coverage in this chapter.

What we want to do is to list in an orderly fashion all nine education incentives, as they influence your individual income tax return. We do so in the aforementioned four stages, as follows:

Stage (1) — Exclusion from gross income,
Stage (2) — Adjustments to total income,
Stage (3) — Deductions from AGI, and
Stage (4) — Exemption of after-tax earnings.

For Stage (1): *Exclusions*, the following three tax code sections apply:

Sec. 117 — Qualified Scholarships.
Sec. 127 — Educational Assistance Programs.
Sec. 135 — Income from U.S. Savings Bonds Used to Pay Higher Education Tuition and Fees.

All three of these sections carry an introductory clause to the effect that: *Gross income does not include . . . .* So, right off, there are certain exclusions from income that do not even show up on your tax return.

As to Stage (2): *Adjustments*, there are only two sections that apply, namely:

Sec. 221 — Interest on Education Loans.
Sec. 222 — Qualified Tuition and Related Expenses.

The statutory wording refers to these items as "deductions." Functionally, yes. But as they are preprinted on page 1 of Form 1040, they are *adjustments to* — or subtractions from — gross income. Deductions, subtractions, adjustments — all have the same effect. They reduce your AGI which ultimately means less tax.

As to Stage (3): *Deductions*, there is only one applicable tax code section. It is—

Sec. 162   — Trade or Business Expenses.

The deduction for education expenses is not clear-cut in the statutory language of Section 162. It is enveloped in such wording as—

A deduction shall be allowed for all ordinary and necessary expenses paid or incurred in carrying on any trade or business.

The education benefit issue is addressed more directly in Regulation § 1.162-5: **Expenses for Education.** We'll focus essentially exclusively on this regulation when we get to this issue below.

As to Stage (4): *Exemptions*, there are three applicable tax code sections. They are—

Sec. 72   — Annuities (Distributions from IRAs).
Sec. 529   — Qualified State Tuition Programs
Sec. 530   — Coverdell Education Savings Accounts

To one extent or another, all three contain the statutory concept that the earnings from these "accounts" . . . *shall be exempt from taxation.* For this exemption to hold, the distributions must be used strictly to pay for qualified educational expenses. Any excess distributions are taxable. None of these matters shows up directly on your return. They show up as disclosure attachments to it.

In Figure 8.1, we give you a brief — very brief — foretaste of how the above nine incentives compare with each other. By listing the statutory word count of each, you can surmise the relative degree of complexity of each incentive. So, now, let's start with Section 117 and work our way through the entire listing in Figure 8.1.

No.	IRC Sec.	EDITED TITLE	Word Count	$ Limit	AGI * Phaseout
Sections of the Internal Revenue Code					
EXCLUSIONS FROM GROSS INCOME					
1	117	Donor-Provided Scholarships	750	None	N/A
2	127	Employer Educational Assistance	1,300	$5,250	N/A
3	135	Higher Education Bonds	2,200	As Justified	$100,000
ADJUSTMENTS TO GROSS INCOME					
4	221	Student Loan Interest	1,800	$2,500	$100,000
5	222	Alternative Tuition Deduction	1,000	$4,000	$130,000
DEDUCTIONS FROM AGI					
6	162	Job Education Expenses	500	As Justified	N/A
EXEMPTIONS AFTER TAX					
7	72	IRA Education Withdrawals	75	As Justified	N/A
8	529	Prepaid Tuition Programs	3,000	As Justified	N/A
9	530	Education Savings Trust	2,500	As Justified	$190,000

* AGI = Adjusted Gross income. Amounts shown are for "Married Filing Jointly". No benefits whatsoever when married filing separately.
"As Justified" means when expenditures do not exceed eligible qualified expenses.

Fig. 8.1 - List of 9 Tax Code Incentives for Higher Education

Donor-Provided Scholarships

A donor is a person or entity that gives/grants money or property to a donee/recipient gratuitously. That is, the donor is sponsoring some worthy cause — such as an academic scholarship or a medical research grant — without the expectation of any consideration (other than sincere gratitude) in return. In most such cases, the donor gets a charitable deduction on his income tax return for his generosity. This, then, raises the question: Does the donee have to pay income tax on the scholarship money that is awarded to him? The answer lies in IRC Section 117.

Section 117: *Qualified Scholarships*, subsection (a): *General Rule*, reads principally as—

> *Gross income does not include **any amount** received as a qualified scholarship by an individual who is a **candidate for a degree** at an* [accredited] *educational institution.*

Be cautioned that the term "any amount" is not unlimited. The term covers only those amounts required for tuition, fees, books, supplies, and equipment for a student's active participation in an established course of instruction. Only these items are construed as scholarship funds.

The emphasized phrase: *candidate for a degree*, is one of two fundamental requirements for excluding scholarship funds from gross income. As per Regulation ¶ 1.117-6(c)(4) such a candidate may be—

(i)   A primary or secondary school student;

(ii)   An undergraduate or graduate student at a college or university who is pursuing studies or conducting research to meet the requirement for an academic or professional degree; or

(iii)   A full-time or part-time student at an educational organization . . . that provides an educational program for full credit towards a bachelor's or higher degree, or offers a program of training to prepare students for gainful employment in a recognized occupation.

Thus, all candidates need not wind up with a college degree, so long as they wind up with a national or state accreditation certificate. For example, a student at an accredited technical school who pursues a course of study to become a mortician is considered a degree candidate. Otherwise, nondegree candidates do not qualify for the Section 117 exclusion.

The second basic qualification for the scholarship exclusion is that the designated funds *be actually used* for qualified tuition and related expenses. Subsection 117(b)(2) defines such expenses as—

(A) tuition and fees required for the enrollment or attendance of a student at an [accredited] *educational organization, and*

(B) fees, books, supplies, and equipment required for courses of instruction at such an educational organization.

These paragraphs (A) and (B) define what are known as "course-related expenses." Other items such as travel, room, board, and incidentals are not considered course-related unless such items are expressly called for in order to complete a specific session or project within the course program. Towards this end, the *recipient* of the scholarship funds must maintain adequate records to substantiate those amounts which he claims are course-related.

The Section 117 exclusion does **not** apply to any portion of amounts received that represent payment for teaching, research, or other services required as a condition for receiving the grant [subsec. 117(c)]. For example, an "educational leave" by an employer (past, present, or future), or any expectation of benefits resulting from the studies and research flowing through to the grantor are deemed compensation for services rendered . . . or to be rendered. The purpose of a scholarship exclusion is to encourage study and proficiency in the subject chosen. It is not for rendering personal services, whether they be to a college, to a nonprofit organization, or to an employer.

Ordinarily, Scholarship grants are not exciting in total dollar amounts. They are not intended to be. They are stipends of $5,000 to $10,000 annually, for knuckling down and getting the credentials sought. Scholarship grants are treated as "educational assistance" only. They are not intended to cover the student's financial support.

There is no statutory limit on the dollar amount of a scholarship grant. Such is the meaning of the term *any amount* bold emphasized in the general rule cited above. Consequently, the amount of grant does not have to be reported on one's Form 1040.

This is what is meant by *exclusion* from gross income, which we depict in Figure 8.2. There is no AGI phaseout requirement, either.

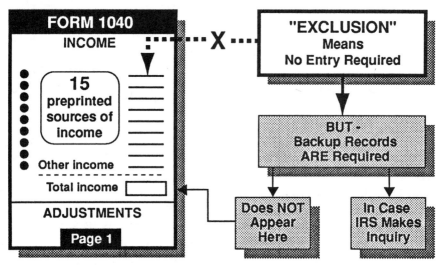

Fig. 8.2 - How Income is Excluded from Your Form 1040

Employer Educational Assistance

Another exclusion from gross income for educational incentives is addressed in Section 127: *Educational Assistance Programs*. Its subsection (a): *Exclusion from Gross Income*, says—

> Gross income of an employee does not include amounts paid or incurred by the employer — of not more than $5,250 — for educational assistance to the employee if the assistance is furnished pursuant to a program which is described in subsection (b).

Immediately, we notice two contrasting features of this exclusion, when compared with Section 117 (the scholarship exclusion). One contrast is the statutory limit at $5,250. An employer can provide more assistance than this, but only the first $5,250 *during a calendar year* is excludable. Any excess amount is tax accountable to the employee and is subject to withholdings by the employer.

The second contrast can be seen only by reading "between the lines." Note that there is no reference to candidate for a degree. In other words, Section 127 applies to nondegree candidates who are seeking to improve their knowledge and skills that will benefit their existing employer.

For the exclusion to be valid (up to $5,250), the employer must establish a *written plan*, make it *nondiscriminatory*, indicate the type of assistance to be provided (tuition, fees, books, supplies, equipment, and other course-related items), and give adequate notification and opportunity to all employees. This is the substance of subsection (b) referenced in subsection 127(a) above.

Benefits not considered to be educational assistance are payments for:

(1) Tools or supplies (other than textbooks) that the employee may retain after completing a course of instruction;

(2) Meals, lodging, or transportation; or

(3) Education involving sports, games, or hobbies, and the use of athletic facilities or equipment which are recreational in nature.

For years, the IRS has fought the $5,250 exclusion benefit. It has taken the position that employer-sponsored educational assistance had to relate directly to each employee's current employment activities or would be denied and therefore taxed. But this was not what Congress had in mind. In 2001 [Economic Growth and Tax Relief Act: P.L. 107-16], Congress reaffirmed the definition of "educational assistance" to be—

The payment, by an employer, of expenses . . . for education of the employee . . . [Subsec. 127(d)(1)].

Other than as mentioned above, there are no restrictions on the kind of education that could be pursued: undergraduate, graduate, job related, or not job related. The legislative intent is to enable workers to advance their general knowledge and skills without incurring additional taxes and a reduction in the take-home pay. The net effect is that the up-to-$5,250 exclusion from gross income is a form of *right* conferred by Congress. It is not a privilege to be sought from the IRS.

Higher Education Bonds

An indirect exclusion for educational expenses pertains to the redemption of Series EE U.S. savings bonds. The "EE" apparently stands for higher Education Expenses at an Eligible Education institution. These are special discounted bonds issued after 1989 to encourage savings for one's education by excluding all or part of the accrued interest from one's Form 1040. The difference between the issue amount and face value, when redeemed, is the accrued interest. Specific conditions for exclusion of the interest are set forth in Section 135.

The full title of Section 135 is: *Income from U.S. Savings Bonds Used to Pay Higher Education Tuition and Fees.* The general rule, subsection (a), reads:

> *In the case of an individual who pays qualified higher education expenses during the taxable year, no amount shall be includible in gross income by reason of the **redemption** during such year of any qualified U.S. savings bond.*

The term "an individual" refers to one who acquires the bonds *after* attaining age 24, who is the sole owner (or joint owner with spouse) at time of redemption, and who uses the proceeds to finance his, his spouse's, or his dependent's higher education. The exclusion is *not allowable if* the bonds are purchased by a parent and placed in the name of a dependent. In addition, married individuals filing separate returns are not eligible for the exclusion.

When the EE bonds are redeemed, the proceeds consist of principal and interest. The amount of principal received is not taxed in any case. It is "return of capital" that you used to acquire the bonds. It is the amount of *accrued interest* which is the target of Section 135. Depending on the length of time holding a bond (5, 10, 15, or 20 years), the amount of accrued interest can be quite substantial. These bonds are ideal for young parents who want to put money aside for their children's college education. While holding the bonds, the accrued interest is not taxable.

When the bonds are redeemed, the excludable amount of interest is determined with Form 8815: *Exclusion of Interest from Series EE and I U.S. Savings Bonds.* This form attaches to Schedule B (Form 1040) as depicted in Figure 8.3. As you can see there, the total EE bond interest is reported, then the excludable portion is subtracted out.

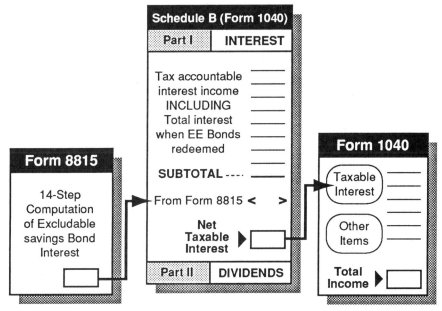

Fig. 8.3 - Concept of Excludable Interest on Series EE Bonds

Student Loan Interest

Another interest-related education incentive is the student loan interest deduction of Section 221. This benefit is an adjustment to your gross income reported on page 1 of Form 1040. Out of ten adjustments listed, the Student Loan Interest (SLI) deduction is the third item. As such, the SLI deduction is more direct than the exclusion of interest for EE bonds.

Section 221 is titled: *Interest on Education Loans*; the general rule under subsection (a): *Allowance of Deduction* reads—

*In the case of an individual, there **shall be allowed as a deduction** for the taxable year an amount equal to the interest paid by the taxpayer* [subject to certain limitations] *on any qualified education loan.* [Emphasis added.]

Subsection (b): *Maximum Deduction*, goes on to say—

Except as [limited by modified AGI], *the deduction allowed by subsection (a) for the taxable year shall not exceed . . . $2,500.*

The term "modified AGI" is your regular AGI (Adjusted Gross Income) modified by adding back certain exclusions and deductions that otherwise would constitute a "double tax benefit."

The term "qualified education loan" in subsection (d) means—

*Any indebtedness incurred by the taxpayer **solely to pay** qualified higher education expenses . . . on behalf of the taxpayer, the taxpayer's spouse, or any dependent of the taxpayer as of the time the indebtedness was incurred. Such term . . . **shall not include** any indebtedness owed to a person who is related to the taxpayer or to any person by reason of a loan under any qualified employer plan.*

The idea here is that the student loan money must be borrowed from a third party (bank, credit union, broker, etc.). Ordinarily, such a party has no personal interest in the student's education. A third party is interested in assuring that the student loan is repaid, both in principal and interest. It is the interest-only portion that is eligible for the deduction. Obviously, only the person legally liable for repayment of the loan, to the extent that it is repaid, can claim the deduction.

A student who is a dependent on his/her parents' (or other claimant's) return is not eligible for the deduction. This is so even though the student may have borrowed the money himself/herself using savings or gifts from family members [subsection (c)]. The rationale for this is that a dependent is being supported in all necessary aspects, including his/her higher education costs.

To establish one's allowable deduction, the *Student Loan Interest Deduction Worksheet* must be used. This is a 10-step worksheet which can be found in the official instruction booklet to Form 1040. After completing the worksheet, you keep it for your records. You enter the result in the adjustment block on Page 1 of your Form 1040. The entry line is signified by the caption: *Student loan interest deduction.* When entered, it adds with other applicable adjustments to reduce your total income (from all sources) to an Adjusted Gross Income (AGI).

Alternative Tuition Deduction

Another education-related deduction against gross income is Section 222. It is titled: *Qualified Tuition and Related Expenses.* This title is duplicative of the term ued in the Hope and Lifetime credits, which we covered in Chapter 7. The difference is that Section 222 is an "alternative" to claiming either or both of those two credits. Whereas the Hope and Lifetime education tax credits focus on low- and middle-income claimants (AGIs under $80,000 married/joint), Section 222 enables claimants with AGIs up to $130,000 to participate.

Towards this end, subsection (a) of Section 222: *Allowance of Deduction*, reads—

In the case of an individual, there shall be allowed as a deduction an amount equal to the qualified tuition and related expenses paid by the taxpayer during the taxable year.

Although this allowance is referred to as a "deduction," it more properly is an *adjustment* to gross income. Congress, in its Committee hearings, clearly intended so. When enacting Section 222 in 2001, it was characterized as an above-the-line deduction. The term "above-the-line" is tax jargon for an adjustment to one's gross income. This is self-evident on page 1 of Form 1040 where a separate line entry: *Tuition and fees deduction*, appears. To help you grasp the above-the-line concept, we present Figure 8.4.

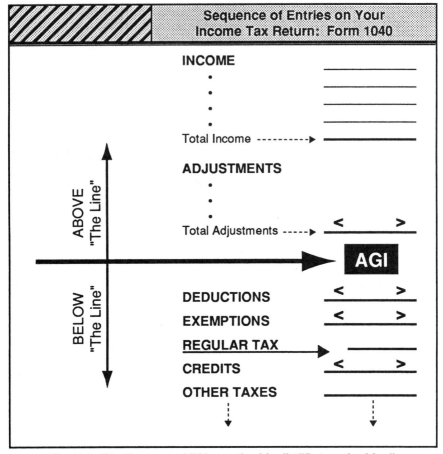

Fig. 8.4 - The Concept of "Above-the-Line" / "Below-the-Line"

In its Committee report on the *Economic Growth and Tax Relief Act of 2001* [P.L. 107-16], Congress stated that—

*The Committee recognizes that in some cases, a deduction for education expenses may provide greater tax relief than the present-law credits. The Committee wishes to maximize tax benefits for education, and provide **greater choice** for taxpayers in determining which tax benefit is appropriate for them.*

The term "qualified tuition and related expenses" has exactly the same meaning as that prescribed in Section 25A(f)(1): *Hope and Lifetime Credits; Definitions*. Once again, the term means those—

tuition and fees required for the enrollment or attendance . . . at an eligible educational institution for [its] *courses of instruction.*

The Section 222 deduction is a **per taxpayer** event. This means that if a taxpayer has more than one qualified student as dependent, the total amount of deductible expenses under Section 222 is limited by prescribed statutory amounts.

The amount of allowable tuition expense deduction/adjustment for the taxable year ranges from $2,000 to $4,000 depending on year and AGI. For years 2002 and 2003, the applicable dollar amount is $3,000 for AGIs not exceeding $130,000 (when filing joint returns). For years 2004 and 2005, the dollar limit is increased to $4,000 for AGIs of $130,000. If the AGI exceeds $130,000 but does not exceed $160,000 (for joint returns), the dollar limit is reduced to $2,000. These limitations are prescribed by subsection 222(b): *Dollar Limitations*.

Job Education Expenses

Many of the above education tax incentives relate to higher education programs leading to recognized degrees, certificates, or credentials. There are other education-type expenditures which also enjoy some — albeit modest — tax benefits. These are what we call: *job education expenses*. Though such expenses do not lead to a degree, certificate, or credential, they lead to higher occupational skills . . . and, ultimately, to higher personal income.

Job education results from attendance at conferences, seminars, workshops, and tours sponsored by trade unions, technical societies, and professional associations. Expenditures for registration, materials, supplies, tools, safety items, travel, and lodging are required. Large employers often pay most of these costs, but not all. Small employers and those having financial difficulties, expect their employees to pay for such "education" on their own. Usually, some written form of attendance certification or completion report is provided, as evidence of the job-related instruction provided.

The allowability of job education expenses derives from Section 162: *Trade or Business Expenses*. Its general rule, subsection (a), reads in part—

*There shall be allowed as a deduction all the **ordinary and necessary** expenses paid or incurred during the taxable year in carrying on **any trade or business**.* [Emphasis added.]

Do you see anything here about education expenses being allowable? Not really, unless you know or have been told that such expenses are covered by the terms "ordinary and necessary" when carrying on "any trade or business." In this regard, Regulation § 1.162-5(a): *Expenses for Education*, is more direct.

This regulation reads in pertinent part as—

Expenditures made by an individual for education (including research undertaken as part of his educational program) . . . are deductible as ordinary and necessary business expenses (even though the education may lead to a degree) if the education—

*(1) **Maintains or improves skills** required by the individual in his employment or other trade or business, or*

*(2) **Meets the express requirements** of the individual's employer, or the requirements of applicable law or regulation, imposed as a condition to the retention by the individual of an established employment relationship, status, or rate of compensation.*

The idea here is that there must be a close relationship between the education expenses incurred and one's **existing** occupation. Education to qualify for one's "first job," or for qualifying for a new job, are not deductible under Section 162. They must qualify under other provisions of tax law.

What type of job related education expenses qualify under Section 162? Answer: They include—

(1) tuition, books, supplies, lab fees, and similar items;
(2) directly related transportation and travel costs; and
(3) other costs such as researching, word processing, or preparing a written paper or report as part of the educational program.

Where do you deduct these expenses? Answer: On Schedule A (Form 1040): *Itemized Deductions*. You identify and enter them in the block captioned: *Job Expenses and Most Other Miscellaneous Deductions*.

Unfortunately, there is a down side to any entry in the miscellaneous block, whether it be educational expense or other. The total of all entries in said block is **reduced** by 2% of your AGI [Section 67: *2-Percent Floor on Miscellaneous Itemized Deductions*].

For example, suppose your AGI is $100,000. Your miscellaneous itemized deductions consist of $5,000 for job education and $2,500 for other miscellany: job and nonjob related. Your 2% AGI floor turns out to be $2,000 [$100,000 AGI x 0.02]. Your net-of-floor allowable is $5,000 + 2,500 – 2,000 = $5,500 (of which $5,000 is your job education expenses). This net-of-floor amount adds to the other itemized deductions on your Schedule A (Form 1040). The total Schedule A amount subtracts — *below* the line — from your AGI. The net effect is that your job education expenses wind up reducing your taxable income.

The roundabout process by which job education expenses become tax deductible is portrayed in Figure 8.5. As is self-evident in Figure 8.5, job education expense deductions are the least direct of all education tax incentives. Still, this deduction process holds up when expenses incurred for other education programs become disqualified. Moreover, there is no statutory limitation to the dollar amount that can be claimed, nor, except for the 2% AGI reduction, is there any AGI phaseout limitation.

IRA Education Withdrawals

Ordinarily, when you make an early withdrawal ("early" means before age 59 1/2) from an IRA plan (traditional or Roth), you are

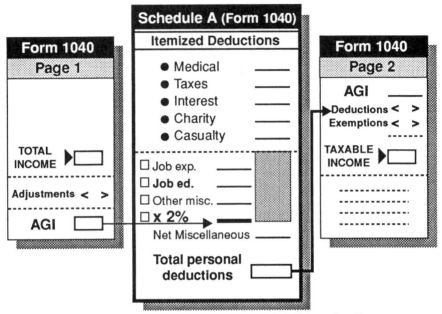

Fig. 8.5 - How the "2% Floor" Operates on Job Education Expenses

subject to a 10% penalty. However, the penalty does not apply if you use the withdrawal proceeds to pay for higher education expenses. Such expenses are those we have previously covered: tuition, fees, books, supplies, and equipment required for enrollment in a recognized educational institution. The enroller may be you, your spouse, your child, or your grandchild.

The authority for this no-penalty benefit is found in Section 72(t)(2)(E). The titles and subtitles to each statutory part of this reference are instructive in and of themselves. Separately, each reads as follows:

Sec. 72 — *Annuities (taxation of distributions from)*
Subsec. (t) — *10 Percent Additional Tax on Early Distribution from Qualified Retirement Plans*
Para. (2) — *Subsection (t) Not to Apply to Certain Distributions*
Subpara (E) — *Distributions from Individual Retirement Plans for Higher Education Expenses*

The substance of subparagraph (E) is that—

Distributions to an individual from [his IRA plan] **to the extent** *such distributions do not exceed the qualified higher education expenses . . .* **shall not be taken** *into account* [under paragraph (1): Imposition of Additional Tax . . . of 10%].

Take particular care to note that nothing is said about the regular tax on the withdrawal amounts. Said withdrawals **are** taxable (particularly for IRAs; less so for Roths). For this purpose, there is a separate line entry on page 1 of Form 1040 which reads—

Total IRA distributions (**a**) _____; *Taxable amount* (**b**) _____

How do you signal to the IRS that the 10% early withdrawal penalty does not apply? Answer: You do so on Form 5329: **Additional Taxes on Qualified Plans (Including IRAs).** In Part I thereof, there are four lines. Each line reads:

1. *Early distributions included in gross income* $_____
2. *Early distributions not subject to additional tax*   _____
   Enter exception number from instructions ___
3. *Amount subject to additional tax. Subtract 2 from 1* _____
4. *Additional tax due. Enter 10% of line 3*   _____

The instructions for line 2 list 10 exceptions to the early withdrawal penalty. Exception No. "08" is identified as—

IRA distributions made for higher education expenses.

Therefore, you enter "08" in the space provided at line 2, before the dollar amount is added. Then follow the instructions on, and accompanying, Form 5329.

Prepaid Tuition Programs

A relatively new incentive in the educational tax domain is the institution of a **prepaid** 5-year tuition program. Doing so is called:

a *Section 529 plan*. The idea is for the parent, in conjunction with other members of the parental family (grandparents, uncles, aunts, cousins) to contribute *cash gifts* to a qualified higher education institution, with the understanding that the distribution of plan assets will go toward a guaranteed program of education to a designated student beneficiary, or to an alternate student in the same family. The educational institution has to establish a "qualified trust" (we'll explain shortly), from which funds are distributed separately for each designated student. The gift amounts are made with after-tax money, but while in the 529 trust, the contributions may generate additional income on their own. As long as the distributions from the trust go to defray the required amounts for tuition, fees, related expenses, including room and board (at on-campus rates), there is no tax consequence to the student beneficiary. If the student receives more than the required amounts for his education, the excess is income taxable to that student.

All of the above is conditionally authorized by Section 529: *Qualified Tuition Programs*. This is a 3000-word tax law. This word count alone should put you on notice that precise qualifications and conditions must be met. Most significant in this regard are its subsections (b) and (c). Subsection (b): *Qualified Tuition Program*, requires that a *qualified trust* be established. Subsection (c): *Tax Treatment of Designated Beneficiaries and Contributors*, enables a contributor (or a combination of contributors) to make the aggregate equivalent of five years of nontaxable gifts to the tuition trust. As of 2002, such aggregate amount could be as much as $55,000 [$11,000/yr x 5 yrs: Sec. 2503(b) and Sec. 529(c)(2)(B)]. The general idea behind Section 529 is portrayed in Figure 8.6.

Subsection (b): *Qualified Tuition Program*, points out that—

> *A person may purchase tuition credits or certificates . . . or make contributions to an account . . . on behalf of a designated beneficiary which entitle the beneficiary to the waiver or payment of* [his/her] *qualified education expenses.*

A "person" may be any member of the student's family related by blood, marriage, adoption, or remarriage, including first cousins,

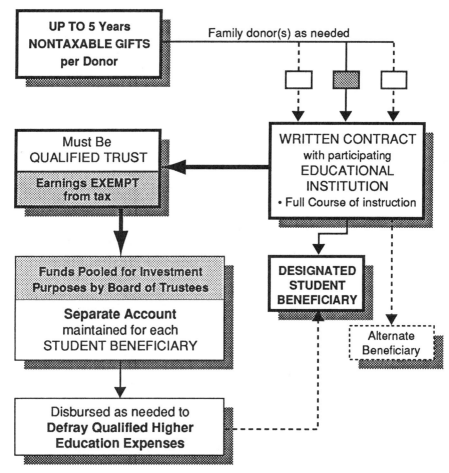

Fig. 8.6 - Concept of "Family Pooling" for Prepaid Tuition Costs

who has a personal and financial interest in the educational success of the student beneficiary.

The real thrust of subsection (b) — in fact, all of Section 529 — is the requirement that a qualified trust be established by the institution sponsoring a prepaid educational program. Before receiving the contributed funds, both the trust and the program must have received an affirmative ruling from the IRS. Among the items to be verified by the IRS are that—

1. The custodian of the funds be a bank, credit union, or other financial institution subject to supervision and examination by the Commissioner of Banking (U.S. or State).

2. The assets of the trust will not be commingled with other property [of the educational institution] except in a common trust fund or common investment fund [for designated student beneficiaries].

3. The program must provide for separate accounting for each designated beneficiary.

4. The program must prohibit any contributor or designated beneficiary from directing or influencing the investment policies of the program.

5. All contributions to the qualified tuition programs be made only in cash.

Education Savings Trust

There is still one more alternative in the domain of tax incentives for education. It is a Section 530 savings trust. Unlike Section 529 which is basically a 5-year *prepaid* tuition account, Section 530 is an up-to-18-year education *savings* account followed by up to 12 years of drawdown for qualified education expenses. Initially (in 1997), Section 530 was titled: ***Education Individual Retirement Accounts***. As such, Section 530 has all of the characteristics of annual contributions to an IRA trust, except that its purpose is not for retirement; it is for *education*. So, in 2001, Section 530 was amended and retitled: ***Coverdell Education Savings Accounts***. For trust accounts initiated after 2001, Section 530 comprises about 2,500 words. Obviously, we can only touch on its highlights.

An education savings account is a **trust** created exclusively for the purpose of paying the qualified education expenses of an individual who is the designated beneficiary of the trust. Contributions to the trust are NOT tax deductible by the contributor.

Hence all seed money used to fund the trust is **after-tax** money. Once in the trust, and other qualifying conditions are met, the *earnings* on the contributed money are tax exempt. When the trust funds are withdrawn and used strictly for the education of the beneficiary, there are no tax consequences to that beneficiary. The concept envisioned by Section 530 is much along the same lines as those portrayed in Figure 8.6.

The essence of Section 530 is that the *income* (earnings on after-tax contributions) from each education savings trust is exempt from tax, provided that—

1. An *Education Savings Trust* be established (in writing) with an IRS-approved financial institution.

2. No more than $2,000 per year (in cash) be contributed to the trust on behalf of its designated beneficiary.

3. The contributions must cease when the designated beneficiary reaches age 18.

4. No part of the trust assets can be invested in life insurance.

5. If the trust assets are not used for qualified education expenses by the time the designated beneficiary attains age 30, the unused assets are released to the beneficiary as taxable distributions.

The most attractive feature of an Education Savings Trust pertains to its more liberal definition of *qualified education expenses*. Said expenses consist of—

(1) those higher education expenses defined in Section 529(e)(3), previously described, **and**

(2) qualified *elementary and secondary* education expenses (kindergarten through grade 12).

Section 530(b)(4): *Qualified Elementary and Secondary Education Expenses* covers such items as—

(i) *tuition, fees, academic tutoring, special needs services, books, supplies, and other equipment . . .* [required] *for the enrollment or attendance of the designated beneficiary at an elementary or secondary public, private, or religious school;*

(ii) *room and board, uniforms, transportation, and supplemental services (including extended day programs) which are required or provided . . . for such enrollment or attendance; and*

(iii) *the purchase of any computer technology or equipment or Internet access and related services, if . . . used by the beneficiary and the beneficiary's family during any of the years the beneficiary is in school.*

As you can sense on your own, "qualified education expenses" under Section 530 cut a much broader swath than any other education tax benefit. Because so, an education trust account can be used as a supplement to any other education expenses not covered by other qualified programs. Furthermore, as long as the beneficiary of the trust is in the same family as the initially-designated beneficiary, a change in beneficiary can be instituted at any time to one who has not attained age 30.

Even the phaseout range for Section 530 contributions is extended beyond the AGI limitations for most other plans. For married taxpayers filing joint returns, the phaseout range is $190,000 to $220,000 of modified AGI.

9

GIFTS, INHERITANCES, & LOANS

In Families Of Modest And Above-Modest Means, The Gratuitous Transfer Of Money And Property To Children and Special-Needs Adults Is Common. Special Tax Laws Apply Which EXCLUDE Such Money And Property From A Recipient's Gross Income. However, Any Income Derived From The Money Or Property Transferred IS Taxable. The Most Beneficial Rule Of All Is The Gifting Of Amounts That Are Below The Threshold Of Gift Taxation: (1) $11,000 Per Year, Per Donor, Per Donee; (2) $1,000,000 Per Donor's Lifetime; (3) Transfers In Trust For Children Under 21; And (4) Payments To Providers Of Educational And Medical Services.

If someone came up to you and handed you a check, made payable to you, for $10,000 and said: "This is yours; there are no strings attached; pay me back if you want to," what would you do?

True; no stranger is going to do this. But close family members can . . . and do. This is particularly likely where there are multiple children of parents, multiple grandparents, and multiple uncles and aunts who are childless.

Many middle-income and modestly-well-off adults provide for the transfer of money or property in the form of gifts, inheritances, and loans to lesser-aged persons in the family domain. These are called *gratuitous transfers*. They are "gratuitous" in the sense that no personal services are performed by the recipient(s), and there is no legally enforceable expectation of payback, even if the arrangement is understood to be a "loan."

Gratuitous transfers among family members are always tax suspect. They raise questions about the motivations involved. Is there some asset secretion or income switching involved? Is there tax avoidance or money laundering taking place? Also, there are uncertainties on the part of the recipient. Does the recipient pay tax on the item(s) transferred? The short answer is "No," but you need to know more than this.

Enter now into the family strategizing world of gifts, inheritances, trust distributions, insurance proceeds, interest-free loans, and other arrangements where modest wealth is transferred from one generation, either across the board or down the line. What ARE the tax implications of family money and property being switched around?

In this chapter, therefore, we address this question head on. We want to touch on the whole gamut of intrafamily transfers and cite the pertinent tax law thereon. We want you to feel confident about the tax treatment of items that you, your children, and other dependents might receive. We also want to point out the tax restrictions that apply, and particularly caution you about a tax trap sleeper — the "kiddie tax" — that could dismay you. The long and short of the strategizing aspects here are: (1) good recordkeeping, (2) no tax gimmickry, and (3) a kind heart.

Be Grateful Always

Let us answer the question that we posed in the opening paragraph of this chapter: "What would you do?"

The first thing you do, of course, is to thank the person who gave you the check. Then look in the lower left-hand corner where the imprinted words *For* or *Memo* appear. If the space is blank, ask what the check is for. Be courteous, gracious, and grateful. All you want to know is the general reason for the check. Is it a gift? Is it an inheritance? Insurance? A loan? Income? What is it? Of course, you'll accept the money, but you want to know its purpose.

Whatever the reason, request the person who signed the check or who handed it to you to fill in the *For/Memo* space. Suggest no more than one or two, maybe three, words. Enter such words as: Gift — grandpa; Inheritance — aunt; Loan — cousin; Life insurance

— stepfather; College tuition — uncle; . . . whatever is relevant and appropriate.

The above is the first thing you do. The second thing you do is photocopy the check. After you cash, trade, or deposit the check, you will not see it again. Once it is canceled, it goes back to the maker of the check. Consequently, you want your own record of the check in photocopy form. The photocopy will show the date it was made, on what institution it was drawn, who signed it, and what it was for. Who knows, someone might question you one day, in an adversarial manner. It could be the IRS; it could be some attorney; it could be a sibling; it could be a family rival; it could be anybody. You just don't want to be caught off guard.

The third thing you do, after endorsing it, is to deposit the check in whatever financial institution you have an account: bank, savings and loan, money market, investment . . . or whatever. Deposit it separately from whatever other deposits you might make at the same time. Your depository institution is a third party, unrelated, whose depository records are above challenge by those who might question or accuse you. When your monthly statement of account comes in, highlight the deposited check, attach its photocopy, and keep in permanent records.

If you expect to receive more than one gratuitous transfer in your lifetime, or over the lifetime of your child or other dependent, repeat the process above for each transfer. Whenever there is "free money," you always want to protect yourself against insidious accusations coming off the wall. You particularly want to be able to prove to the IRS that the money was not ill-gotten . . . nor is it tax accountable!

Gifts and Inheritances

In the mandated world of tax impositions, the term *gross income* is frequently used. This term is a synonym for "tax accountable income." A Form 1040 filer must disclose all sources of gross income (on page 1) before any adjustments, deductions, exemptions, or credits are taken into account. But if a particular type of income is expressly excluded from gross income, it does NOT show on your Form 1040. It is excludable income, meaning TAX

FREE. Such is the case with gratuitous transfers, of which gifts and inheritances are prime examples.

The relevant tax low on point is IRC Section 102: *Gifts and Inheritances*. Its subsection (a), *General Rule*, says—

*Gross income **does not include** the value of property acquired by gift, bequest, devise, or inheritance.* [Emphasis added.]

Subsection (a) is not open ended. It is limited by subsection (b), *Income*, which says—

Subsection (a) shall not exclude from gross income:
  (1)   the income from any property referred to in subsection (a), or
  (2)   where the gift, bequest, devise, or inheritance is of income from property, the amount of such income.

Here, in succinct terms, we have the fundamentals of taxation on all financial transactions. The issue is: **capital versus income.** Section 102(a) makes it clear that the transfer of *capital* (value or principal) is not taxable to the recipient. Similarly, Section 102(b) makes it clear that all *income* from capital, whether in the same transfer or not, **is** taxable. So important is this concept that we present a depiction of it in Figure 9.1. We had Figure 9.1 in mind when we urged that you ascertain the reason and source of money or property that may be transferred to you (or to your child, or to a dependent) gratuitously.

Section 102 uses the phrase: *gift, bequest, devise, or inheritance.* The term "gift" refers to the conveyance of money or property out of pure generosity, affection, respect, admiration, or charitable impulse. A "bequest" is a specific assignment of money or personal property to an heir or nonheir in accordance with one's Last Will and Testament. A "devise" is the transfer of real estate by any legal means recognized in the state where the real property is situated. An "inheritance" is a birthright or blood line transfer of money or property after the death of the taxable owner. In all of these transfers, the clear separation of capital and income is mandatory.

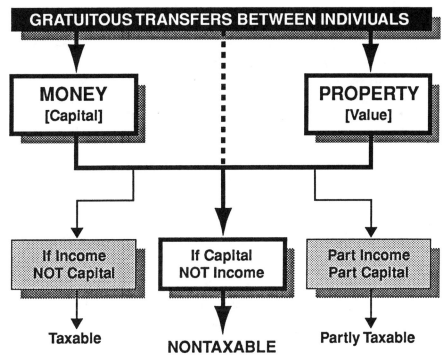

Fig. 9.1 - Separation of Capital & Income for Taxability Purposes

Regulation ¶ 1.102-1(a): *General rule,* repeats the above and points out that separate rules apply to prizes, awards, scholarships, and fellowships. Then, Regulation ¶ 1.102-1(b): *Income from gifts and inheritances,* states clearly that—

> *The income from any property received as a gift, or under a will or statute of descent and distribution shall not be excluded from gross income.*

Regulation ¶ 1.102-1(c): *Gifts and inheritances of income,* also says—

> *To the extent that any gift, bequest, devise, or inheritance is paid, credited, or to be distributed out of income from property, it shall be considered a gift, bequest, devise, or inheritance of income from property.*

The above regulations support our depiction in Figure 9.1. Repeating the message therein, for any gratuitous transfer, effort must be made to distinguish between capital and income. Who makes this effort? Answer: the *transferor*. The transferee (recipient) may make inquiry, but has no first-hand knowledge of the tax source or tax character of the money or property being transferred. If the transferor fails to make the distinction, the transferee has to do so, from the best information available.

Distributions from Trusts

By far, the most contentious tax characterization problems of gratuitous transfers are distributions from family trusts. All kinds of exotic-sounding trusts are involved. Parents, grandparents, and uncles/aunts who are modestly well off are fascinated by the aura and mysticism of the word "trust." They regard a trust as a means of perpetuating its contributory capital via the generation of income by the trust. The result is that any distributions to designated beneficiaries are a *mixture* of capital *and* income. The distinction can be made clear, if the trust instrument specifies the distributive intent.

Let us illustrate the trust tax character problem. To present the idea more convincingly, let us use two illustrations: Example 1 and Example 2.

In Example 1, the trust instrument specifies that Alicia (a granddaughter) is to receive $60,000. The instrument specifies that the $60,000 is to be paid in one lump sum or in not more than three installments. Under these conditions, the $60,000 of payments is excluded from Alicia's gross income. As such, it is not treated as a gift of income from property. How so? A special tax law says so.

The special rule on point is Section 663(a)(1): *Exclusions: Gifts, Bequests, Etc.* This rule says—

Any amount which, under the terms of the governing instrument, is property paid or credited as a gift or bequest of a specified sum of money or of specific property, and which is paid or credited all at once or in not more than 3 installments . . . shall not be included in [a recipient's] gross income.

The illustrative situation is different in Example 2. Here, Boris is the grandson who is designated to receive $25,000 per year for four years. No distinction is made as to how the payments are to be characterized: capital or income. During Year 1, the trust earned $16,000 in income; Year 2 it earned no income; Year 3 it earned $10,000 income; and in Year 4, the trust had an operating loss. For this example, Boris is the only beneficiary. How are his distributions tax treated?

As to Year 1, Boris has to pay income tax on $16,000. In perpetual type trusts, income is always distributed first. In Year 1, Boris also gets $9,000 in capital (25,000 − 16,000 = 9,000). The capital part is NOT TAXED. In Year 2, the entire distribution of $25,000 is capital, as no income was generated by the trust in that year. In Year 3, the income portion is $10,000 and $15,000 is capital. In Year 4, the distribution of $25,000 is all capital. This is because the income losses to a trust are not passed through to the beneficiaries until the year in which the trust terminates.

It is not our intention here to wander off into the taxation of trust distributions. We just want you to be alert to the "capital vs. income" characterization problem. A properly managed trust can make the distinctions clear by issuing to each beneficiary a **Schedule K-1 (Form 1041)**. This schedule is titled: *Beneficiary's Share of Income, Deductions, Credits, Etc.* This schedule provides line entries for 25 types of income, deductions, and credits; has 3 line entries for "final year" for loss passthroughs; and has 6 blank lines for indicating distributions of capital. All capital entries in these blank lines should be trustee identified as: NONTAXABLE.

Life Insurance Proceeds

Another way of transferring money to other members of the family is via life insurance. A life insurance contract is a form of trust, of which the insuring company is the trustee. One or more persons other than the insured (or his estate) are designated as beneficiary recipients of the insurance proceeds. The beneficiaries are treated as receiving gratuitous transfers of capital equal to the stated face value of the policy If the policy pays off by reason of death of the insured, there is no statutory limit to the amount of capital excludable from gross income. Such is the substance of Section 101(a)(1).

Section 101(a) is titled: *Proceeds of Life Insurance Contracts Payable by Reason of Death.* Its paragraph (1) is the General Rule, which reads—

> *Except as otherwise provided . . ., gross income does not include amounts received (whether in a single sum or otherwise) under a life insurance contract, if such amounts are paid by reason of the death of the insured.*

The "except as otherwise provided" clause pertains to (1) transfers of policies for valuable consideration, (2) payments at a date later than death, and (3) flexible premium contracts before January 1, 1985. It is the **face value** only that is excluded from gross income.

Particularly note in the statutory wording of Section 101(a) that there is no limit to the amount of exclusion from gross income. The face amount of a policy could be $100,000; $700,000; $3,000,000 . . . or more. Whatever the face amount, it is not taxable to the recipient.

Subsection 101(a) addresses the face capital value only. Subsection 101(c) addresses *Interest*, which is income. This subsection says—

> *If any amount excluded from gross income by subsection (a) is held under an agreement to pay interest thereon, the interest payments shall be included in gross income.*

Thus, if a $100,000 face value policy paid $104,680 at time of death, $100,000 would be capital and $4,680 would be income. Life insurance companies usually make the separation clear. They do so via IRS Form 1099-R.

Form 1099-R is titled: *Distributions from Pensions, Annuities, Retirement or Profit-Sharing Plans, IRAs, Insurance Contracts, etc.* Its importance to the recipient focuses on boxes 1, 2a, and 7. Box 1 is captioned: *Gross distributions*; box 2a is: *Taxable amount*; and box 7 is: *Distribution code.* There are about 30 different code designations in the *Instructions for Recipient* that accompany Form 1099-R. The one pertinent here is Code 4: *Death*. This means that the difference between box 1 and box 2a is excluded from gross income.

Section 101 comprises about 3,750 words of text. We have cited only about 60 words of the 3,750. The uncited words, together with court rulings thereon, cover an entire industry of estate planning arrangements using life insurance as a transfer mechanism.

Gift Taxation Explained

Everyone who has filed Form 1040, 1040A, 1040EZ, or 1040NR knows that there is an income tax. But not everyone knows that there is a *gift tax*. It's there for anyone to access and read, in the Internal Revenue Code. It encompasses Sections 2501 through 2505. If a taxable gift is made, Form 709: *U.S. Gift Tax Return*, is required.

Section 2501(a): *Taxable Transfers by Gift*, imposes a gift tax at a rate directed in Section 2502, after taking into account certain exclusions from gift tax outlined in Section 2503. The significance of Section 2501(a) is that—

A tax . . . is imposed each calendar year on the transfer of property by gift during such calendar year by an individual, resident or nonresident. [Emphasis added.]

Note the emphasis on the term "individual." Trusts, corporations, partnerships, or other entities cannot make gratuitous gifts. A "resident" is any person living in the U.S. who is either a U.S. citizen or a foreign citizen. A "nonresident" is a foreign citizen who is not living in the U.S. at the time of gifts.

Gift tax rates *start* at 18% and graduate up to 48% for taxable gifts over $3,000,000. However, before any gift tax is actually paid, the statutory one-time exclusion of $1,000,000 has to be cumulatively exhausted. Once the exclusion is exhausted, Section 2502(c): *Tax to be Paid by Donor*, states clearly that—

The tax imposed by section 2501 shall be paid by the donor.

In other words, the recipients of gifts (whether the amount is $10,000 or $1,000,000) are free and clear of all gift taxation. Being unaware of this is one of the great missed opportunities for shifting money around among family members. With good forethought and disciplined use of *annual exclusions* (as distinguished from the "one-time" exclusion), substantial amounts of money, cumulatively over many years, can be gratuitously gifted.

Subsection 2501(a)(2): *Transfers of intangible property*, provides an interesting commentary. It says—

Except as provided in paragraph (3), paragraph (1) [cited above: "A tax . . . is imposed"] *shall not apply to the transfer of intangible property by a nonresident not a citizen of the U.S.*

In other words, if you have family relatives living abroad who are foreign citizens by birth or otherwise, each such donor can make an unlimited dollar amount of gifts to a U.S. person. There is absolutely no U.S. tax consequence to a foreign donor, whatsoever. Nor are there any tax consequences to U.S. recipients. The "paragraph (3)" exception pertains to former U.S. citizens who gave up their citizenship and expatriated to a foreign country to avoid U.S. taxation.

Exclusions from Gift Tax

There is a whole range of gift opportunities which are excluded from the gift taxation process. Specifically, there are four such domains, namely:

I — The one-time lifetime/deathtime exclusion of from $1,000,000 (beginning in 2002) to $3,000,000 (in year 2008, if not otherwise altered by Congress).

II — The annual exclusion of up to $11,000 per donee, with no limit to the number of donees.

III — Cumulative gifts to minors up to the age of 21, when held in a custodial account until that age.

IV — Direct payments to educational institutions and medical care facilities on behalf of **any** family or nonfamily member. The number of such "on behalfs" is unlimited.

We summarize these four exclusion domains in Figure 9.2 by adding the tax code sections that specifically allow them.

Category II illustrates, more than any other, the "missed opportunities" of continuous gifting without concern for taxation on the donor. For example, if there were seven worthy donees in a family, and $11,000 per year were made to each for 10 years, a total of $770,000 (7 donees x $11,000/yr x 10 yrs) could be gratuitously transferred without incurring any gift tax. This is the essence of Section 2503(b)(1), to wit—

The first $11,000 of gifts made to any person by the donor during the calendar year . . . shall not be included in the term "taxable gifts." [The $11,000 amount applies to year 2002 and is inflation indexed thereafter.]

Category III is more complex than we have indicated in Figure 9.2. It involves the transfer of money, securities, insurance policies, annuity contracts, or other property into what is popularly known as a *Uniform Gifts to Minors Trust* (UGMT). This is an informal account with a regulated financial institution whereby the parent of a child under age 21 can be the legal custodian of the child's funds. The custodian, however, must never be the donor of the transferred funds. This is because the donor must release all dominion and control over the funds when in a UGMT. As a result, most gifts to minors tend to be by grandparents or by other relatives who have no minor children of their own. Hence, no formal trust documentation needs to be prepared inasmuch as all qualified financial institutions use the same standard format. Said format is simply the establishment of a custodial account flagged "UGMT," and showing the date of birth of the child. Monthly or quarterly account information is sent to the legal custodian of each child's separate account . . . for tracking purposes.

When a UGMT earns income (interest, dividends, capital gains) — as it should — who pays tax on that income?

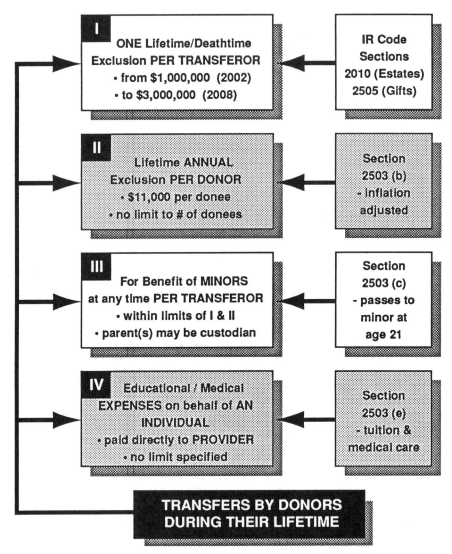

Fig. 9.2 - Statutory Exclusions Before Any Actual Gift Tax Occurs

Answer: Technically, the child does. The child owns the money and property in the account; the custodian does not. However, if the child's parent is the custodian, either the parent or the child can pay the tax. If the child is under age 14, it is usually more practical that the parent pay the tax. At age 14 or over, it is more beneficial that the child pay the tax. His/her tax rates are likely to be lower than those for the parents.

Treatment of "Gift Loans"

Another form of gratuitous family transfers has to do with low-interest, no-interest loans which turn out to be gifts. The tax law that addresses these and *other* friendly loan arrangements is Section 7872. Its full title is: ***Treatment of Loans with Below-Market Interest Rates.*** This section was enacted in 1984 and now comprises about 3,500 words. In addition to gift loans, it addresses demand loans, term loans, employee loans, shareholder loans, capital transaction loans, continuing care loans, tax avoidance loans, and all other below-market loans. The term "below market" means a loan at a rate of interest below the Applicable Federal Rate (AFR) published monthly by the IRS. The AFRs are short term (under 3 years), mid term (3 to 9 years), and long term (over 9 years).

The difference between the AFR interest and the stated loan interest, if any, is called: *forgone interest.* The idea behind Section 7872 is that the forgone interest amount is treated as being transferred from the lender to the borrower which, unless expressly gifted to the borrower, is retransferred back to the lender as imputed interest income. This treatment produces — or can produce — both gift tax and income tax implications. Our focus in this chapter, however, is on two particular exceptions that are beneficial to intrafamily arrangements.

The first exception is subsection 7872(c)(2): ***$10,000 De Minimis Exception for Gift Loans Between Individuals.*** This subsection reads in principal part—

> *In the case of any gift loan directly between individuals, this section shall not apply to **any day** on which the aggregate outstanding amount of loans between such individuals does not exceed $10,000 . . . [provided] the loan is not used for the purchase or carrying of income-producing assets.*

Thus, at any time during the year, a $10,000 loan can be gifted and forgiven, including its forgone interest.

The second exception is subsection 7872(d)(1): *Limitation on Interest Accrual for Purposes of Income Taxes Where Loans Do Not Exceed $100,000*. This subsection reads in principal part—

In the case of a gift loan directly between individuals, the amount treated as retransferred by the borrower to the lender as of the close of any year shall not exceed the borrower's net investment income for such year . . . [provided] *the aggregate amount of such loans does not exceed $100,000.*

As we read this, if a relative loaned a family member $100,000 at a rate 3% below the applicable AFR rate, for example, and earned $15,000 in net investment income therefrom, only $3,000 ($100,000 x 0.03) would be treated as imputed interest income to the lender. If the stated interest rate were 5% (for an AFR rate of 8%), the $5,000 of bona fide interest earned could be treated as a gift to the borrower. If there were no net investment income at all (such as if the loan money were used to buy a personal residence or to pay down existing mortgage debt), there would be no imputed interest income to the lender. The $5,000 stated interest could be gifted, together with $5,000 of principal. This would reduce the balance of principal to $95,000 due. The process would be repeated each year until the balance is fully amortized or gifted.

Avoiding the "Kiddie Tax"

When gratuitously transferring money and property among family members — especially to minor children — there's a "tax sleeper" out there. We want to forewarn you about it. It is called the *Kiddie Tax*. It applies expressly to children under age 14 who have investment income (interest, dividends, capital gains) of more than $1,500 for the calendar year. The kiddie tax rule (IRC Section 1(g)(2)) requires that any child with investment income who—

has not attained the age of 14 before the close of the taxable year, and either parent of such child is alive at the close of the taxable year . . .

shall be taxed as if the investment income were the parent's income. In other words, a child who ordinarily would be in the 10% tax bracket has to pay tax at his parents' tax rate of 25% to 35%.

Let us exemplify.

Suppose that, when your first child was born, your parents (the child's grandparents) set up a custodial account and transferred to it $11,000 per year for each of five consecutive years. At age 5, the child would have $55,000 of investable money. Suppose this money earned 5% per annum. That would be $2,750 [55,000 x 0.05] of investment income. If the child could prepare his own tax return, and allowed you as the parent to claim him as a dependent, his income tax would be $200 [($2,750 – $750 special exemption) x 10%]. But under the kiddie tax rule, his tax is mandated to be $825 [$2,750 x 30% parent's tax rate] . . . four times higher.

Can you avoid the kiddie tax? Yes, you can. How?

By using the child's money to acquire shares in one or more mutual funds which invest in different maturity *state and local municipal bonds*. These forms of investment are popularly called: "Tax Free Muni Bond Funds." True, their yields are not exciting: order of 2% to 5%. But they ARE TAX EXEMPT! No kiddie tax returns are required.

The Federal tax law on point is IRC Section 103: *Interest on State and Local Bonds*. Its subsection (a): *Exclusion*, reads—

Except as [otherwise] *provided, gross income does not include interest on any State or local bond.*

The term "interest" applies to the obligated yield on the underlying bond debt. If you hold individual bonds, you receive interest. If you hold shares in a mutual fund, you receive dividends. In the yield parlance of municipal bonds, interest and dividends (except for capital gains) are synonymous.

Through gratuitous transfers (gifts, inheritances, trusts, insurance, loans) from various family members, some children can accumulate — from birth on — quite substantial assets. If the accumulations reach potentially in the range of $100,000 or more, investing in tax-free municipal bond funds is definitely an attractive consideration. Being of low tax-free yields (2% to 5%), such bonds do not fluctuate in market value to the extent that common stock and corporate bonds do. Consequently, the capital gain distributions from a mutual fund of municipal bonds seldom exceed 1% or 2% of fund assets. This means that, roughly, one can expect about $1,500 of capital gains for every $100,000 of asset value. These capital gains *are* taxable. Of the capital gain amount, a minor child gets a special $750 exemption. The net effect is that your child winds up paying 10% on $750 (1,500 – 750) or about $75. To this $1,500 in capital gains there could be added about $5,000 in tax-free dividends. Thus, for a total investment income of $6,500, the tax is a negligible $75. This is an effective tax rate of slightly over 1%.

Strategically, therefore, putting children's "college money" into tax exempt mutual funds can make sense. This is especially true if gratuitous transfers are made to the child over a period of many years — say, from birth to age 25 or so. Tax-free accumulations, even at low annual yields, compound quite strikingly over many years.

10

SAVINGS BEHIND THE LINES

> Various Rules Permit Exclusions From, Or Reductions Of, Gross Income Reported On Form 1040. Examples Are ELECTIVE DEFERRALS And FRINGE BENEFITS By Employees Who Participate In Employer-Sponsored Programs. When Self-Employed, One Can Elect To ACCELERATE Or DEFER Income, Capital Expenditures, And/Or Operating Expenses. Tax On Capital Gains Can Be Softened By Electing The Year Of Transaction, Maximizing "Return Of Capital" (Which Is Tax Free), And Using Losses For Strategic Offsets. Cumulative Unallowed Passive Activity Losses Are Usable When The Entity Is Sold In A Fully Taxable Transaction.

Saving family taxes is an "opportunity thing." That is, you troll for opportunities that exist under ordinary tax rules, rather than responding solely to special incentives that come and go with the political tides. Our reference to ordinary rules pertains to those which have been on the books for many years and which are pretty well ingrained into the pubic psyche. There are opportunities there, but you tend to miss them. You have to know where and how to look. And, you have to take a new look each year.

For example, take a look at page 1 of Form 1040 about midway down, where it is bold-labeled: **Income**. If you haven't previously counted them, there are **15** different lines for entering various sources of income. They are totaled at the line captioned:

*This is your **total income**.*....................................._____

Have you ever read down all 15 of the income lines on your Form 1040 carefully? For those on which you make entries, have you ever probed "behind the lines" for what you might do to legitimately omit entries or reduce the amount you report on these lines?

You realize, of course, that what does not appear in the 15 lines, or appears in reduced amounts, automatically means less tax to pay. In other words, if your total true spendable income is $100,000, and by pre-entry exclusions and deductions you can reduce the total reportable to $75,000, say, there automatically will be less tax to pay. This is so, irrespective of your filing status and the number of dependents you claim.

What we want to do in this chapter, therefore, is to indicate a methodology for your trolling behind the lines, on your own. The key for doing so is to identify those lines which offer potential, and eliminate those which do not. It is not a matter of expecting to find grandiose tax loopholes; it is a matter of dogged tax digging. While you dig, ask yourself: "If this behind-the-line item is authorized by law, why am I not using it?" It may be that the item does not apply, or it may not be significant in your case. Still, you want to be alert to discovering any tax savings that might arise.

The 15 Income Lines

It would be best if you had a copy of your own latest-filed Form 1040 at your fingertips. But, in case such is inconvenient at the moment, we present in Figure 10.1 an edited listing of the 15 income lines on Form 1040. The sequence we present is identical to that on the official form. It is the wording that we have edited. Of the 15 items listed, we have Xd seven as presenting nil opportunity for tax saving efforts. Those that are not Xd provide "behind the lines" opportunities.

There is one item of wording that you should particularly notice when glancing at Figure 10.1. We group label the 15 lines: *Gross Income*. Yet, the bottom line on both the official form and our Figure 10.1 uses the term: *Total income*. What is the difference? Why do *we* use "gross income"?

FORM 1040	Page 1	Year
Filer Identity	Filing Status	Exemptions Claimed

	GROSS INCOME	
1	Wages, salaries, etc. Attach Form(s) W-2	☐
2	**Tax-exempt** interest _____ Taxable interest	☐
3	Ordinary dividends	X
4	State / local income tax refunds	X
5	Alimony received	X
6	Business income / loss. Attach Schedule C	☐
7	Capital gain / loss. Attach Schedule D	☐
8	Other gains or losses. Attach Form 4797	☐
9	IRA distributions. Taxable amount	X
10	Pensions & annuities. Taxable amount	X
11	Rental real estate, partnerships, trusts. Attach Sch. E	☐
12	Farm income / loss. Attach Schedule F	☐
13	Unemployment compensation	X
14	Social security benefits. Taxable amount	X
15	Other income. List type _____	☐
	Add the above. This is your **total income**	☐

Fig. 10.1 - The 15 Income Lines on Form 1040

Answer: Because the Internal Revenue Code uses the term: Gross income; it does not use the term: Total income. Subchapter B of Chapter 1 of the tax code is titled: Computation of Taxable Income. Part I thereunder is titled: *Definition of Gross Income, Adjusted Gross Income, Taxable Income, Etc.* The definitions of these terms are prescribed in Sections 61 through 68. Nowhere in these eight sections is the term "total income" defined.

Section 61 defines gross income as—

Except as otherwise provided in this subtitle, gross income means all income from whatever source derived, including (but not limited to) the following items . . .

Clearly, the sense of this definition — *all income from whatever source derived* — implies total income. But any such implication is altered the moment you focus on the opening clause: *Except as otherwise provided . . .* This clause refers to **35 items** that are specifically excluded from gross income. If you can exclude one or more of the designated items from gross income, you automatically reduce the bottom line tax you pay. Hence, we list the 35 excluded items for you in Figure 10.2. You might want to glance down the list, and do some independent research on your own. We cite the IRC Code Sections to aid in your research.

Internal Revenue Code: Chapter 1: Subchapter B: Part III - Items Specifically Excluded From Gross Income			
Sec.	Item	Sec.	Item
101	Certain death benefits	123	Insurance receipts for living exp.
102	Gifts and Inheritances	125	Cafeteria elective plans
103	Interest on municipal bonds	126	Certain cost-sharing payments
104	Compensation for injuries	127	Employer educational assistance
105	Receipts under health plans	129	Dependent care assistance
106	Employer provided health plans	130	Certain liability assigments
107	Rental value of parsonages	131	Certain foster care payments
108	Income from discharge of debt	132	Certain fringe benefits
109	Lessee improvements to property	134	Certain military benefits
110	Certain construction allowances	135	Higher education savings bonds
111	Recovery of tax benefits	136	Energy conservation subsidies
112	Combat pay: Armed Forces	137	Adoption assistance programs
114	Extraterritorial income	138	Medicare + Choice MSA
115	State & muncipality income	139	Disaster relief payments
117	Qualified scholarships	140	Cross references to other Acts
118	Capital to a corporation	NOTE: These IRC section titles are are edited and abbreviated. See IRC for full titles and text. Contact a tax professional if one or more items would be useful to you.	
119	Employer furnished meals/lodging		
120	Group legal plan receipts		
121	Gain on sale of residence		
122	Disability military retirement		

Fig. 10.2 - Listing of Items Specifically Excluded From Gross Income

First Look: Form(s) W-2

Here's a fast start example of what we mean by digging behind the lines. Take a look at the very first income entry on Form 1040. That line reads—

Wages, salaries, tips, etc. Attach Form(s) W-2.

By digging behind the lines, have you ever looked at and read all of the small print captions to the boxes on the face of Form W-2?

Excluding the boxes for state and local income tax matters, there are 14 boxes on Form W-2. Box 1 is captioned: *Wages, tips, other compensation.* This is the amount reported to the IRS. It is possible that said amount is **less than** that which you actually received. For example, box 10 (year 2002) is captioned: *Dependent care benefits.* When entered in box 10, up to $5,000 can be excluded from box 1.

Whatever amount is in box 1, together with other W-2s you may have, or your spouse has, must show up as one aggregate amount in the first income entry on Form 1040. The higher this amount, the higher your tax; the lower the amount, the lower your tax. Make sense?

But you don't want to cut your actual income just to reduce taxes, do you? You want to cut only the amount that your employer reports to the IRS in box 1. How can this be done? This is where **box 12** (year 2002) comes in.

Pull out your latest Form(s) W-2 that you kept for your records. This should be: *Copy C for **Employee's Records**.* A tiny-print notation somewhere thereon says: *see instructions on back of Copy C* (or on an attachment to Copy C). Then look at the instructions for box 12. There you'll find 18 code symbols: "A" through "V". Skim-read down these 18 items, mentally ticking off those which might apply in your case.

Now, stop for a moment. Did you notice any items that started with the term: *Elective deferrals . . .?* There are five such items in a row: D, E, F, G, and H. There is also a 6th one at S: *Employee salary reduction contributions to a section 408(p) SIMPLE (**not** *included in box 1).* Section 408(p) is titled: Simple Retirement Accounts (hence the term "Simple").

Our point here is that there are certain statutory elections — 401(k) plans, for example — whereby you can defer current box 1 income for taxing later. The "later" has to be associated with some employer-sponsored pension, profit-sharing, stock bonus, savings, or deferred compensation plan. Generally, these plans permit up to $11,300 per employee, per year (as of 2002) to be salted away for the future. If your spouse also works for an employer with a deferred compensation plan, she/he too can defer $11,300. That's up to $22,600 (depending on the plan) on which you and your spouse can avoid current-year taxation. If you are age 50 or over, you are allowed to make up for earlier-year less-than-maximum contributions to a plan, at the rate of an additional $1,000 per year. Have you checked with your employer(s) on this?

If your employer offers any form of elective deferral (or deferred compensation) plan, and you are not a participant in the plan, we have to ask: "Why aren't you a participant?" Saving for retirement is a long, long-term affair. It is never too early to start. If you cannot contribute the maximum amount allowed, contribute what you can. Then discipline yourself to increase to the maximum within three to five years. Whatever you contribute to a qualified plan will definitely reduce the box 1 amount on Form W-2. This, in turn, proportionately reduces your income tax.

Other Box 1 Reductions

In addition to retirement-type plans, there are other items that can reduce the entry amount in box 1. For spotting these items, you must focus on **box 12**. Unlike the other boxes on Form W-2, there is no descriptive caption at box 12. Instead, box 12 consists of four associated boxes designated as: 12a, 12b, 12c, and 12d. Each of these "associated" boxes displays a vertical line for separating the code symbol from its dollar amount. Although enlarged in size here, each such box looks like this—

Code	Amount

It is most important, therefore, that you observe carefully the code symbol in each of the box 12 associates. As recently stated, these symbols extend from Code A though Code V.

Not all entry amounts in the box 12 associates are reductions in box 1. For example, Code C reads—

*Cost of group-term life insurance over $50,000 (**included in box 1**.)*

If such life insurance is not over $50,000, your employer-paid premiums are not in box 1. We use this example to alert you to the importance of reading the fine-print information that accompanies each of the code symbols: "A" through "V". You particularly want to search for and note those symbols that say— "not included in box 1" or "nontaxable."

On this searching note, we call to your attention the following symbols and their coverings:

Code J — *Nontaxable sick pay (**not included in box 1**).*

Code L — *Substantiated employee business expense reimbursements (**nontaxable**).*

Code P — *Excludable moving expenses reimbursements paid directly to employee (**not included in box 1**).*

Code T — *Child adoption benefits (**not included in box 1**).*

And, just to keep you on your toes, Code V reads—

*Income from exercise of nonstatutory stock options (**included in** boxes 1, 3 (up to the social security wage box) and 5).*

There is also **box 14** that you should look at carefully. This box on Form W-2 is captioned: *Other*. This box is one big blank space. Its vertical height is $2^1/2$ times that of any other numbered box. Here the employer reports "odds and ends" for which no box 12 code symbol is assigned. Both taxable and nontaxable amounts can be shown. Because so, **you** (as the employee) have to inquire as to which is which. For example, box 14 might show an entry for union (or professional) dues, payments for uniforms, educational assistance, voluntary after-tax contributions to a pension plan, makeup contributions to a pension plan, or whatever else the employer wants to communicate to his employees.

Small Business Elections

Lines 6 and 12 in Figure 10.1 have similarities to each other. They represent the net income of small businesses conducted by individuals. These are sole proprietorship businesses: single owner types. Line 6 addresses Schedule C (1040): *Profit or Loss from Business*, whereas Line 12 addresses Schedule F (1040): *Profit or Loss from Farming*. The Schedules C and F are *self-employment* tax forms.

Unlike the gross wages of employment (reduced perhaps by elective deferrals and fringe benefits), Schedules C and F transfer the **net** income earned: not the gross. Schedule C or Schedule F net income can be a loss as well as a profit. The possibility of a loss means that a small-business owner can elect to accelerate or defer portions of his gross income, portions of his capital outlays, and/or portions of his operating expenses. He can make these elections to produce a net income of his choice. However, if the net income is too low or is negative (meaning: loss) year after year, tax suspicions arise. Is he in business solely for the tax benefits, or is he in business to make a profit? If losses are frequent, they can be disallowed when transferred from Schedules C or F to Form 1040 (IRC Sec. 183: *Activities Not Engaged in for Profit*).

The best example we know of for a small-business tax election is Section 179. This section is titled: *Election to Expense Certain Depreciable Business Assets*. Its subsection (a): *Treatment as Expenses*, reads—

A taxpayer may elect to treat the cost of any section 179 property as an expense which is not chargeable to capital account. Any cost so treated shall be allowed as a deduction for the taxable year in which the section 179 property is placed in service.

The term: "Section 179 property" means any tangible property — machinery, equipment, vehicles, tools, etc. — used in a trade or business with a useful life of more than one year. Ordinarily, these items have to be capitalized and subject to depreciation allowances over a period of three, five, ten, or more years.

Subsection (b)(1): *Dollar Limitation*, sets the "applicable amount" for the election at $25,000 in year 2003 and thereafter. Subsection (b)(3): *Limitation Based on* [Net] *Income of Trade or Business*, says, in essence, that you cannot use the $25,000 election to drive your net income negative. But you can target it to zero. On both Schedules C and F there is a deduction item captioned as—

Depreciation and section 179 expense deduction.

You can repeat the Section 179 election each year that it is applicable.

In addition to the above, there are other fringe-benefit-type opportunities on Schedules C and F. We generalize these in Figure 10.3. The idea behind Figure 10.3 is that you, as the sole business owner, have some control over your gross receipts/sales and your deductible operating expenses. By this, we are NOT implying any form of "cooking the books." For example, if you intend to add to inventory, do so at the beginning of the year rather than at the end of the year. Any ending inventory is tied up capital. It actually **increases** your tax! High ending inventory is the motivation for promotional sales and other cost markdowns (for damaged goods, older-model merchandise, and outright giveaways).

Self-Employed "Adjustments"

If, when conducting a Schedule C or F business, you do so for livelihood purposes, you will have a net profit most of the time. After all, it is the profit motive that results in income that supports you, your spouse, and your dependents. This is called "self-employment" . . . or being self-employed.

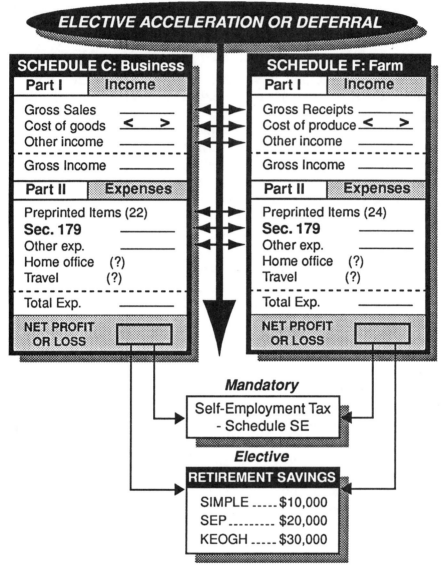

Fig. 10.3 - The Elective Aspects of Schedules C and F

As a self-employed individual, there are three particular tax savings benefits that do not show up on Schedules C or F. They show up as *adjustments* to your gross income that is totaled on page 1 of your Form 1040. These adjustments/deductions are:

- One-half of self-employment tax
- Self-employed health insurance deduction
- Self-employment retirement plan (3 options)

When the net profit is reduced on Schedules C and F, the above three adjustments also are reduced. When a net profit is shown, an instruction at that line reads—

> *If a profit, enter on* **Form 1040, line** _____, *And ALSO on* **Schedule SE, line** _____.

Schedule SE (Form 1040) is titled: *Self-Employment Tax.* The SE tax is a combination of social security and medicare taxes. When the amount of the SE tax is computed, there is a subsidiary line on Schedule SE designated as: *Deduction for one-half of self-employment tax.* Enter on **Form 1040, line** _____. The purpose of this deduction (adjustment) is to put self-employed individuals on a par with employed persons whose employers pay one-half of the social security/medicare tax. In reality, a self-employed person gets a slight advantage in that his SE tax is figured on net earnings, rather than on gross compensation as in the case of an employee.

Section 162(*l*)(1)(B) authorizes the deduction of 100% (for year 2003 and thereafter) for health-care insurance costs. The purpose here is to put self-employed persons on a par with corporations, which can deduct 100% of the health insurance costs for employees.

In the savings-for-retirement arena, a self-employed person may elect one of three options. He may have a SIMPLE 401(k) plan; he may have a SEP 408(k) plan; or he may have a KEOGH 401(c) plan. A SIMPLE is treated as a deferred compensation plan; a SEP is treated as a profit-sharing plan; a KEOGH is treated as two separate plans: (a) *pension* **and** (b) *profit-sharing*. Under a SIMPLE, up to about $10,000 can be contributed; under a SEP, up to about $20,000 can be contributed; and under a KEOGH, up to about $30,000 can be contributed. These are the strictly approximate amounts that we show in Figure 10.3.

We say "up to about," because the rules on retirement savings keep changing every year. Congress — and the IRS — cannot seem to make up their minds. Nevertheless, the trend is towards establishing an inflation-adjusted maximum contribution base (net personal service earnings) of $160,000. For each separate plan, there would be a maximum defined contribution percentage (between 5% and 20%) for self-employed persons. Whatever the post-2002 year outcome may be, all authorized retirement savings contributions are — and will continue to be — deductible against gross income.

Transactional Gains & Losses

Lines 7 and 8 in Figure 10.1 go hand in hand. In each case, an attachment schedule is required. For line 7, the attachment is Schedule D (1040): *Capital Gains and Losses*. For line 8, the attachment is Form 4797: *Sales of Business Property*. Because in both cases (Schedule D and Form 4797) capital is returned tax free, these activities are characterized as "transactional." It is the capital advanced that produces the gain or loss. It is not personal service as in the case of Form W-2, Schedule C, or Schedule F.

In any capital transaction, some asset must be acquired, improved, or modified, and subsequently sold or exchanged. Upon sale or exchange, gain or loss results. The gain is taxable; a loss is deductible, but certain limitations apply. The return of capital is not taxed. The rationale is that you paid tax on this capital before you were able to invest it.

Your behind-the-lines strategy is to recover the maximum possible amount of capital, tax free. This means keeping — and updating — good records on your part. Your records should include (a) cost of acquisition, (b) cost of improvements or modifications, (c) cost of defending or perfecting legal title, (d) cost of local assessments and security systems, and (e) expense of sale or exchange (including commissions, fees, and document taxes). All of this recordkeeping effort is grouped under the Schedule D/Form 4797 columnar heading of:

Cost or other basis, plus improvements and expense of sale.

The "cost or other basis, etc." is the kind of tax information that you have to create and keep track of on your own. Your broker is not required to do it for you. And, certainly, the IRS will not do it for you. The IRS has no knowledge of your cost information until you report the sale or exchange on your return.

In the meantime, when a capital asset is sold, the IRS is notified of the *gross sale price*. It is notified **each time** that a capital transaction has taken place. It is then up to you — not the IRS — to compute your gain or loss on **each transaction**.

If, after tallying your gains and losses on Schedule D, there is a net *long-term* capital gain, you enjoy preferential (lower) tax rates (20% or so). If the net is short-term gain, ordinary rates apply (28% plus). If the net is a capital loss, short-term or long-term, only $3,000 is deductible that year. Any excess net loss over $3,000 is carried forward to subsequent years.

Form 4797 differs from Schedule D in two important respects. One difference is a separate columnar accounting called:

Depreciation allowed or allowable since acquisition.

This amount is ADDED TO the gross sale price under the long-standing rule of: **Depreciation recapture**. This catches many business-property sellers by surprise. Recapture means that if you have been aggressive in your depreciation, depletion, and/or amortization writeoffs over the years, your aggressiveness will come back to haunt you.

The second difference between Schedule D and Form 4797 is the application of Section 1231: *Property Used in the Trade or Business* (some 1,300 words). If the net tally of Form 4797 is a loss (short-term, long-term makes no difference), Section 1231 *converts* that loss from capital loss to an *ordinary loss*. There is no $3,000 current-year limitation. You can deduct the entire loss against all other sources of positive income that you have otherwise entered on Form 1040. Any net long-term gain on Form 4797 is transferred onto Schedule D. The relationship between Schedules D, Form 4797, *and other forms and schedules* is depicted in Figure 10.4. Do not underestimate the opportunities on Schedule D.

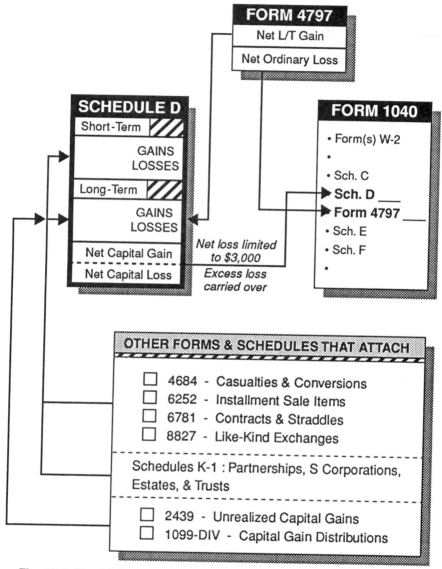

Fig. 10.4 - The All-Inclusive Role of Schedule D for Capital Transactions

Supplemental Income/Loss

Line 11 in Figure 10.1 reads officially as—

Rental real estate, royalties, partnerships, S corporations, trusts, etc. Attach Schedule E.

Schedule E, in turn, is titled: ***Supplemental Income and Loss***. It is a rather formidable form: some 60 entry lines, columnized. It consists of five parts, namely:

Part I — Income or Loss from Rental Real Estate and Royalties

Part II — Income or Loss from Partnerships and S Corporations

Part III — Income or Loss from Estates and Trusts

Part IV — Income or Loss from Real Estate Mortgage Investment Conduits

Part V — Summary: Including Net Farm Rental Income

Of these, only Parts I and II present any significant opportunities for behind-the-line savings for individuals.

Under certain conditions, Part I: Rental Real Estate, permits up to $25,000 as a current-year loss writeoff. The amount of this loss which is not subject to phase-out can be used to offset other positive sources of income on Form 1040. The law on point is Section 469(i): ***$25,000 Offset for Rental Real Estate Activities***. Subsection 469(i)(3)(A): *Phaseout of Exemption*, says—

In the case of any taxpayer, the $25,000 amount . . . shall be reduced (but not below zero) by 50 percent of the amount by which the adjusted gross income of the taxpayer for the taxable year exceeds $100,000.

In other words, for AGIs in excess of $150,000, the permissible loss writeoff evaporates entirely.

Part II of Schedule E: Partnerships and S Corporations, constitutes the primary domain of *pass-through* entities. These are trade or business operations which are structured to give front-end writeoffs in the form of ordinary losses, and give back-end writeons in the form of capital gains. Except for the day-to-day material participants therein, these entities are classed as: *passive activities*.

As such, they are subject to the disallowance rule of Section 469: *Passive Activity Losses Limited.*

There is one salvation to the passive loss limitation rule of Section 469. As per its subsection (b), any unallowed losses for a given year may be carried over to the next taxable year . . . and to the next . . . and to the next . . . etc. See Figure 10.5 for the carryover idea involved. Cumulatively tracking these "passive loss carryovers" (as they are called) is a real opportunity to tax dampen the back-end write-on years. Applicable in this regard is Section 469(g): *Dispositions of Entire Interest in Passive Activity . . . shall be treated as a loss which is not from a passive activity.* In other words, when the property is sold, the cumulative unused passive losses are treated as "addition to basis." This automatically reduces the amount of capital gain . . . and its tax.

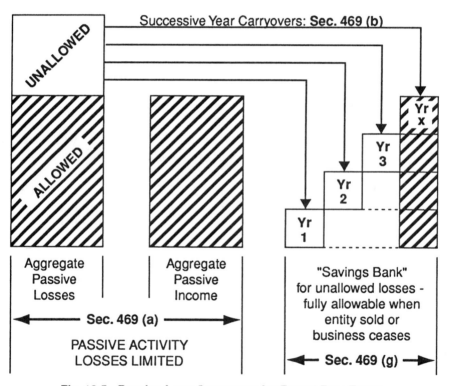

Fig. 10.5 - Passive Loss Carryovers for Rental Real Estate

Tax Law Fussiness: Ebb & Flow

What makes a tax return confusing and often complex is the occasional on-again, off-again "fine tuning" of a tax law. Much of this is Congressional fussiness to satisfy the political whims of the day. The basic law itself is not materially affected, and the procedural aspects thereto stay much the same. It is just that certain dollar amounts, percentage rates, and applicable years offer short-term teaser benefits to targeted groups of the taxpaying public. A good example of the on-off teasing is the JGTRRA '03: *Jobs and Growth Tax Relief Reconciliation Act of 2003*. We think that selected examples from this '03 Act will help you better understand the objectives of this chapter, as well as of this book.

In Chapter 4, we acquainted you with the child tax credit and its procedural aspects. For year 2002, the credit was $600 for each child under age 17. At that time, there were scheduled increases (in $100 increments) to reach $1,000 in 2010. In May 2003, when JGTRRA was enacted, the credit jumped to $1,000 for years 2003 and 2004 **only**. In 2005, the originally-scheduled increases-to-$1,000 resume. (The year 2004 is a Presidential election year.) Otherwise, nothing in Chapter 4 is significantly altered.

Another political fuss point is the Section 179 expense election for physical assets (machinery, equipment, computers) purchased and used in a small business. We commented on this earlier in this chapter. The pre-May '03 statutory amount was $25,000. After May '03, the allowable amount jumps to $100,000. The jump is effective for years 2003 through 2005. In 2006 and thereafter it reverts to $25,000 again. This type of back and forth "dollaring" is what drives tax planners and tax professionals wild.

A more general ebb and flow observation pertains to the treatment of net long-term capital gains. In 1997, Congress reduced the long-term rate from 28% to 20% where it was supposed to be fixed for good. Along comes JGTRRA, whereupon the rate was reduced further to 15% for years 2003 through 2008. (You are aware, of course, that 2008 is another Presidential election year.) In year 2009 and thereafter, the fixed-for-good 20% rate resumes. The concept of preferential tax treatment for capital gain income was first introduced in 1954. The maximum effective rate then was 35%.

Yet, the tax accounting principles for determining the amount of capital gain has not changed since that time.

What has changed is the annual "adjustment creep" caused by monetary inflation. In 1913 when the federal income tax was constitutionalized, $1 then would buy **20 times** what the same dollar buys in 2003. In other words, a 2003 dollar is worth about 5% of a 1913 dollar. [The official indexing on this is: 9.9 (1913) ÷ 185.8 (2003) = 0.0533, about 5%.] The measure most often used for determining erosion of the dollar is the *Consumer Price Index for all Urban Consumers*: CPI-U.

It was not until 1992 that Congress finally adopted CPI-U indexing as official tax policy. It first expressed the policy in Section 1(f)(3): *Cost-of-Living Adjustments*. Illustrative portions thereof read—

The cost-of-living adjustment for any calendar year is the percentage (if any) by which—

   (A)   the CPI for the preceding calendar year exceeds
   (B)   the CPI for calendar year 1992.

The year 1992 was supposed to be the common reference base for all subsequently designated CPI-indexed tax laws. Not all tax laws (there are about 10,000 of them) have been so designated. Only about 60 or so have been CPI designated. But even as few as 60 separate indexing laws can cause anxiety and frustration on every family tax return, year after year. Consequently, it seems to us that. some **grand simplification** of the tax code is sorely needed, if Congress and the IRS truly want to make the tax laws more taxpayer self-compliant . . . and more taxpayer friendly.

11

DEDUCTION PHASEOUTS & AMT

Strategizing Becomes More Difficult As Parental Incomes Increase Above $150,000 Married Joint ($75,000 Married Separate). This Is Because Three Sets Of PHASEOUT Rules Apply. Such Rules Are Directed At (1) Itemized Personal Deductions, (II) All Personal Exemptions, (III) The AMT Exemption, And (IV) Most Nonrefundable Credits. Before Your "Adjusted Tax" Can Be Established, You May Face Another Set Of Rules Called: AMT (Alternative Minimum Tax). The Net Result: TWO TAXES Are Computed. You Pay The HIGHER Of The Two, Not The Minimum. The AMT Can Be A Perennial Cross To Bear For Middle-Income Taxpayers.

For most parental returns, a common attachment is Schedule A (Form 1040). This schedule is titled: *Itemized Deductions*. It covers such items as medical expenses, property taxes, mortgage interest, charitable contributions, job expenses, and other miscellaneous deductions. At the very bottom of this schedule, before the deduction items are totaled, there is a phaseout computation that may apply. If the phaseout does apply, it reduces the amount of your allowable Schedule A deductions. Such reduction, in turn, *increases* your regular tax.

Differently, though somewhat similarly, there is — or may be — a phaseout of your personal exemptions. The phaseout threshold is based on a different AGI amount (adjusted gross income) from that of Schedule A. But the end effect is the same. Phaseout reduces your allowable personal exemptions which, in turn, increases your regular tax.

And, if the ordinary phaseouts do not increase your tax enough, there is a special add-on tax called: AMT. The letters "AMT" stand for: Alternative Minimum Tax. The term "alternative minimum" is a misnomer. It is actually an alternate *maximum* tax.

Once you compute your regular tax *and* the AMT tax, various credits (to reduce that tax) may apply. For each credit computation, there is a phaseout procedure of its own (as explained in previous chapters). Again, the phaseout effect is to increase your regular tax.

Accordingly, in this chapter we focus on page 2 of Form 1040. We start at the very top line: Adjusted Gross Income [AGI], and work our way down, as pertinent, to: *Total tax*. This total is your regular tax, *plus* your AMT add-on (if any), *minus* allowable credits. We have a lot to tell you about the AMT tax, and why we think it will only get worse. Fortunately, not all parental returns face AMT. Nevertheless, we do not want you to be caught by surprise. Nowadays, AMT affects a broad spectrum of middle- and upper-middle-income taxpayers.

The Schedule A Phaseout

Schedule A (1040) consists of between 25 and 30 entry lines (depending on how you count the blank lines). The very last preprinted line is captioned: *Total Itemized Deductions*. At this line, you are asked—

*Is Form 1040, line [AGI], over [$135,000, **for example**] (over [$67,500] if married filing separately)?*

☐ *No. Your deduction is not limited.*
☐ *Yes. Your deduction may be limited. See* [instructions] *for amount to enter.*

The instructions provide you with an: *Itemized Deduction Worksheet.* You are told to fill out the worksheet, enter the results on Schedule A, then keep the worksheet for your records. It is a 10-line, 280-word worksheet. The gist of this worksheet is as follows:

[1]   Total everything on Schedule A as though there were no phaseout.
[2]   Subtract from [1] the sum of your (a) medical expenses, (b) investment interest, (c) casualty losses, and (d) allowable wagering losses.
[3]   Multiply the result of [1] – [2] by 80%.
[4]   Subtract from your AGI the *applicable amount* designated on the worksheet for the taxable year for your filing status.
[5]   Multiply the result of [4] by 3%.
[6]   Enter the *smaller of* [3] or [5].
[7]   Subtract [6] from [1]. Enter as your Schedule A total. Then follow instructions for entry on Form 1040.

The IRS-provided worksheet (as edited and abbreviated above) is the fulfillment of Section 68 of the IR Code. The section title is: *Overall Limitation on Itemized Deductions*. Its subsection (a): *General Rule*, reads—

*In the case of an individual whose adjusted gross income exceeds the applicable amount, the amount of the itemized deductions otherwise allowable for the taxable year shall be reduced by **the lesser of**—*

(1) 3 percent of the excess of the adjusted gross income over the applicable amount, or
(2) 80 percent of the amount of the itemized deduction otherwise allowable for such taxable year.

Subsection 68(b) defines the "applicable amount." This amount started at $100,000 in 1991, and, after indexing for inflation, it rose to $137,300 in 2002 ($68,650 if married filing separately). Each year, the applicable amount changes and is preprinted at the last line on Schedule A. It appears in the question form that we cited on page 11-2. On page 11-2, we used the amount of $135,000 strictly as an example. We wanted to focus on the procedural aspects of the phaseout process, rather on a specific amount for a specific year. The larger applicable amount applies to *all filers* except married filing separately.

The idea behind Section 68 is that, as your AGI increases beyond the applicable amount, you will wind up paying more tax than you would have without Section 68. Let us illustrate.

Suppose your AGI (with $365,000 of capital gains) turns out to be $515,000 (150,000 ordinary income plus 365,000 capital gains). Assume the applicable amount to be $135,000. Your Schedule A deductions before Section 68 are $40,000, say. Your phaseout amount would be the "lesser of"—

3% x (515,000 – 135,000) = $11,400
OR
80% x $40,000 = $32,000.

In the great majority of high AGI cases, the 3% phaseout rule produces the lesser reduction. For the illustration presented, the allowable Schedule A deduction would be $28,600 (40,000 – 11,400): NOT $8,000 (40,000 – 32,000). Without the capital gains in the AGI, the 3% reduction in Schedule A would be a mere $450 (0.03 x (150,000 – 135,000)).

Phaseout of Personal Exemptions

Not satisfied with phasing out the Schedule A deductions, Congress (and the IRS) have carried their phaseout fervor to your personal exemptions (you, your spouse, children, and dependents). It's all there in the IR Code at Section 151(d)(3): *Exemption Amount; Phaseout.*

The substance of Section 151(d)(3) reads—

In the case of any taxpayer whose [AGI] . . . *exceeds the* [phaseout] *threshold amount, the exemption amount* **shall be reduced by** . . . *2 percentage points for each $2,500 (or fraction thereof) by which the taxpayer's* [AGI] . . . *exceeds the threshold amount. . . . In no event shall the applicable percentage* [of reduction] *exceed 100 percent.* [Emphasis added.]

The "threshold amount" — the AGI at which phaseout begins — is indexed to inflation. For 2002, these AGI levels were:

$206,000 — married filing jointly
171,650 — head of household
137,300 — single
103,000 — married filing separately

As you can see, "married filing separately" encounters the most severe phaseout consequences. The reason is that such persons would prefer to file as two singles: 2 x $137,300 = $274,600.

At the line on page 2 of Form 1040 where you enter your total exemption amount, a preprinted caution says—

If line _____ is over $103,000 [for 2002], *see the worksheet on page* _____ [of the instructions] *for the amount to enter.*

This instructional reference leads you to the: **Deduction for Exemptions Worksheet** — which you keep for your records. This is a 9-line, 300-word form which computes the amount you subtract from your otherwise regular exemption. The instructions on this worksheet further caution you that, **if your excess AGI** (over the threshold amounts) is more than $61,250 married filing separately, or more than $122,500 for all others: **Enter zero** for your exemptions.

As you probably have already sensed on your own, phaseout is a big revenue producer for the IRS. Also, as you can sense, there is nil coordination or consistency between the Schedule A phaseout (which starts at $137,300 for married joint) and the exemptions phaseout (which starts at $206,000 for married joint) [year 2002].

Other Phaseout Inconsistencies

In prior chapters, we addressed the phaseout rules which curtailed the tax benefits of certain credits. We are not going to rehash these rules. But, for inconsistency comparisons, we are going to list the AGI thresholds (for married filing jointly) where the phaseouts begin. Accordingly, these AGI thresholds are:

- Adoption credit — $150,000
- EE bond exclusion — $116,000

- Child credit — 110,000
- Education credit — 102,000
- Student loan interest — 100,000

Aside from the inconsistency among these threshold AGIs, matters are made worse for these credits. A "modified" — meaning: *enhanced* — AGI is used to accelerate the wipeout of the benefits. And there is no uniformity among the modifying items that are added to your ordinary AGI for phaseout purposes. Our conclusion is that if your ordinary AGI is more than the amounts below, you might as well bypass seeking most of the above credits. Generally, the credit-abandonment thresholds are:

$150,000 — married filing jointly
112,500 — single or head of household
 75,000 — married filing separately

There **are** some credits which are *not* subject to AGI phaseout rules. The only one that we have discussed is the Dependent Care Credit in Chapter 3. There are others listed on page 2 of your Form 1040. For example, the foreign tax credit, the general business credit, and the credit for prior-year minimum tax, though subject to limitation, are not subject to ordinary phaseout. The "limitation" we speak of here is the regular tax liability limitation of Section 26: *Limitation Based on Amount of Tax.* In other words, since all the above-mentioned credits are nonrefundable, your total credits allowable for the year cannot exceed your regular tax plus the AMT tax. In some cases, (child adoption, for example), the unusable portion of any nonphasedout credit may be carried forward. Generally, though, for AGIs exceeding our thresholds above, the term "nonrefundable" means no credit is likely.

Introduction to AMT

As mentioned earlier, the letters "AMT" stand for: Alternative Minimum Tax. This terminology derives from the title of Section 55, which is: *Alternative Minimum Tax Imposed.* The subsection (a): *General Rule* is—

*There is hereby imposed (**in addition to any other tax** imposed)
a tax equal to the **excess (if any) of**—
(1) the tentative minimum tax for the taxable year, over
(2) the regular tax for the taxable year.* [Emphasis added.]

In other words, the focus of computation is on the EXCESS of
AMT over your regular tax.

To give you a handle on where we are heading on the subject of
AMT, we present Figure 11.1. Especially note that our Item 6 is the
regular tax to which subsection 55(a)(2) above refers. Also note our
Item 8 in Figure 11.1. This is where the AMT tax ADDS to your
regular tax. The two together become your *Enhanced Tax* (before
any credit offsets). Can you not sense the added complexity when
AMT is imposed?

Meanwhile, be informed that AMT Section 55 consists of about
2,400 words of statutory text. This section was enacted in 1978 and
has been amended **16 times** since then! This number of
amendments should tell you — it does tell us — that Section 55 is
convoluted, complex, and confusing. It is the kind of law that
makes it best to have a tax professional test its applicability in your
case, or have a professional software program that does the work
and thinking for you.

Initially, the intent of Section 55 was to insure that upper-middle
and high-income taxpayers pay at least some minimum amount of
tax. The intent was — and still is — to **add back** a number of
itemized deductons and tax preferences that one may have taken to
arrive at his (comparatively low) regular taxable income. The
addbacks produce what is called: *Alternative Minimum Taxable
Income* (AMTI). From the AMTI, certain exemption amounts
may be deducted, after which *two* separate flat-tax rates apply.
There is a flat 26% rate for those whose adjusted AMTI is $175,000
or less. A 28% flat rate applies to all others. If married filing
separately, this two-rate threshold is $87,500. The AMT flat-rate
tax that you have computed is then compared with your regular tax.
Should your regular tax be higher, there is no AMT tax. Should
your AMT computation be higher than your regular tax, the excess
amount becomes your AMT add-on.

	Starting at Top of page 2, Form 1040		
1	Your ORDINARY AGI		——
	Ordinary itemized deductions	——	
	PHASEOUT AMOUNT I	< >	
2	Reduced itemized deductions		< >
3	REVISED AGI (Item 1 less item 2)		▭
	Ordinary personal exemptions	——	
	PHASEOUT AMOUNT II	< >	
4	Reduced personal exemptions		< >
5	Taxable income (Item 3 less item 4)		——
6	REGULAR TAX (see instructions)		▦
7	Alternative Minimum Tax: Form 6251		——
8	Adjusted tax (Add Items 6 and 7)		▭
	Credits subject to phaseout	——	
	PHASEOUT AMOUNT III	< >	
	Credits NOT subject to phaseout	——	
9	TOTAL OF CREDITS ALLOWABLE		< >
10	Tax After Credits (Item 8 less Item 9)		▦
	Self-employment tax: Schedule SE		
	Other taxes		
	Household employment tax: Schedule H		
11	Total Tax: Add Items 10 on down		▭

Fig. 11.1 - Sequence of Events When the AMT Tax Applies

Introduction to Form 6251

To understand the subtleties of a complex tax law, it is often better to get an official copy of the IRS form that addresses that law. In the case of AMT, there is such a form. It is Form 6251: *Alternative Minimum Tax — Individuals*. It is composed of some 57 entry lines, and is accompanied by about 10,000 words of instructions. Form 6251 is arranged into three distinct parts, namely:

Part I — Alternative Minimum Taxable Income – 28 lines
Part II — Alternative Minimum Tax – 7 lines

Part III — Computation Using Maximum Capital Gains
         Rates – 22 lines

Our depiction of the correlation between Form 1040 (regular tax) and Form 6251 is presented in Figure 11.2. As so indicated in that figure, the very first entry line on Form 6251 is your "Reduced AGI." By following the first bold arrow in Figure 11.2, you can see that the Reduced AGI is the third line on **page 2** of Form 1040. Because this third line is not specifically identified on Form 1040, we have chosen to assign it an identity of our own.. Officially, its line caption is—

Subtract line_____ [Itemized deductions]
from line_____ [Your AGI]

This Form 1040 third line **precedes** all of your personal exemptions. In other words, you get no AMT benefit whatsoever for your personal exemptions!
         Line 1 of Form 6251 reads—

*If filing Schedule A (Form 1040), enter the amount from Form
1040, line _____ [above], and go to line 2.*

Starting at line 2 through line 27, there are 22 **add-back** and four **subtraction** adjustments. Some of these adjustments are self-explanatory on Form 6251 itself. Most, however, require reference to the 8-page, separately printed: *Instructions for Form 6251.*
         The very last line (28) in Part I of Form 6251 is captioned—

Alternative Minimum Taxable Income [AMTI].
*Combine lines 1 through 27. (If married filing separately . . .,
see the instructions.)*

In every case, your AMTI is greater than your regular taxable income. Generally, it is one-and-a-half to *three* times greater. It depends on your particular add-ons and subtractions. If married filing separately, and your AMTI exceeds $173,000 (for year 2002), 25% of the excess over $173,000 becomes another add-back.

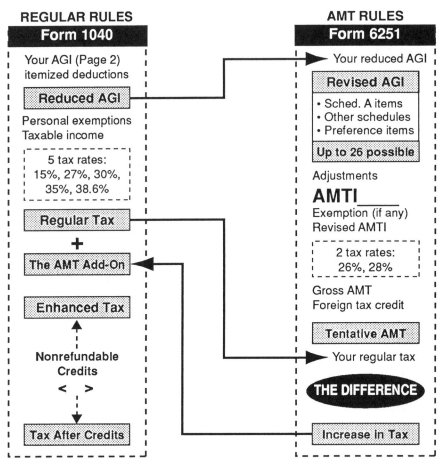

Fig. 11.2 - The "General Idea" of AMT Law for Increasing Your Tax

The net result of the above is that AMT is brutal tax business. The only concession to AMT-vulnerable taxpayers is the allowance of statutory exemptions against the AMTI.

AMT Exemptions & Phaseouts

If you were to use your AMTI and filing status, and go to the regular tax rate schedules, you'd be alarmed at the result. Sensing a taxpayer's revolution at AMT, Congress (via Section 55(d)(1)) has authorized an exemption amount before applying the AMT tax rates. For year 2002, the exemption amounts were:

Married filing jointly	$49,000
Single or head of household	35,750
Married filing separately	24,500

Sadly, we observe that Congress has become addicted to phaseouts (and the revenue they produce). The AMT exemption amounts in Section 55(d)(1) are phased out in Section 55(d)(3). The specific wording on point is—

*The exemption amount of any taxpayer **shall be reduced** (but not below zero) by an amount equal to 25 percent of the amount by which the [AMTI] of the taxpayer exceeds—*

$150,000 . . . [for married filing jointly],
112,500 . . . [for single or head of household], *and*
75,000 . . . [for married filing separately].

For example, suppose as a married joint filer, your AMTI is $265,000. Your phaseout amount would be—

($265,000 − 150,000) x 25% = $115,000 x 25% = $28,750.

So, instead of the $49,000 potentially allowable exemption amount, your exemption would be reduced to $20,250 (49,000 − 28,750). The Form 6251 instructions provide an: ***Exemption Worksheet*** for going through the phaseout process.

Part II of Form 6251

The very first line in Part II of Form 6251 addresses the phaseout of the AMT exemption amounts that we discussed above. You are instructed on the form to do this—

*If line 28 [your AMTI] is **over the amount shown** [in Part II] for your filing status, see the instructions.*

After subtracting any applicable exemption from your AMTI, you arrive at a *revised* AMTI. At this "subtract line" on Form 6251, there follows an 80-word preprinted instruction. This instruction is extensive and confusing. You have to read it carefully several times to get the gist of what is being imposed.

The essence of the Form 6251 instruction is that two, separate, flat-tax rates apply. If your revised AMTI is $175,000 or less (87,500 for married separate), multiply your revised AMTI by 26%. If more than $175,000, multiply by 28%, then subtract $3,500. The instruction also says (in effect) that if you have net long-term capital gains on Schedule D (1040), go to Part III before entering your AMT tax in Part II. In Part III, after exhausting your preferential capital gain rates, you then apply the AMT rates.

The bottom line on Part II of Form 6251 reads—

Alternative Minimum Tax. Subtract line _____ [your regular tax] *from line* _____ [your tentative AMT]. *If zero or less, enter -0-.* [Otherwise] *Enter here and on Form 1040, line*_____ [AMT. Attach Form 6251].

The sequence of events leading up to the final AMT amount is presented in Figure 11.3. We have editorialized the official wording of Part II so that it is a "stand alone" for instructional purposes. For example, our line 1 in Figure 11.3 does not actually appear in Part II. It appears in Part I. Yet, to better "see" the computational mechanics of Part II, you have to start with your Part I AMTI (Alternative Minimum Taxable Income).

Line 4 in Figure 11.3 is what we gave you the gist of above. For instructional convenience, we caption that line: **Gross AMT tax.** Officially, the instructions are much different. Without any editing whatsoever, they read—

• *If you reported capital gain distributions directly on Form 1040, line 13, or you had a gain on both lines 16 or 17 of Schedule D (Form 1040) (as refigured for the AMT, if necessary), complete Part III on page 2 and enter the amount from line 57 here.*

Form 6251	Part II	ALTERNATIVE MINIMUM TAX	
1	Your Part I **AMTI**		_____
2	Exemption amount (after phaseout, if any)		< >
3	Revised AMTI (subtract line 2 from line 1)		_____
4	Gross AMT tax (see Form 6251 instructions)		▬▬▬
	☐ Check if Part III used	////////////	
5	AMT Foreign tax credit		< >
6	Tentative minimum tax (subtract line 5 from line 4)		▪▪▪▪▪▪▪
7	Enter regular tax from Form 1040, **REDUCED**		< >
	BY ☐ Amount on Form 4972, if any	/////////	
	BY ☐ Amount on Form 1116, if any	/////////	
8	**AMT.** Subtract line 7 from line 6		
	Enter here and on Form 1040	⬜	

x x x x x x x x x x x x x x x x x x x x x x x x x x x x x x x x x x x x

Fig. 11.3 - The Form 6251 Sequence From AMTI to AMT

- *All others. If line 30 is $175,000 or less ($87,500 or less if married filing separately), multiply line 30 by 26% (0.26). Otherwise, multiply line 30 by 28% (0.28) and subtract $3,500 ($1,750 if married filing separately) from the result.*

See what we mean? Reading and rereading caution is required.

The use of Part III, where applicable, is intended to preserve your lower capital gains rate (10% to 20%) before applying the 26%/28% AMT rate. Otherwise, the only opportunity to reduce your AMT is the foreign tax credit (line 5 in Fig. 11.3) should it be applicable. But even this credit is figured differently for AMT.

Line 7 in Figure 11.3 also requires caution when following the official instructions. They read—

Enter your [regular] *tax from Form 1040, line 42 **minus** any tax from Form 4972 and any foreign tax credit from Form 1040, line 45* [or from Form 1116].

Form 4972 is titled: *Tax on Lump-Sum Distributions from Qualified Retirement Plans.* Form 1116 is titled: *Foreign Tax Credit — Individuals.* It is rare that these two forms would apply to the same individual for the same taxable year, but they could.

The real essence of Part II is that you compare your regular tax with the tentative AMT tax. If your regular tax is equal to or higher than the tentative AMT, there is no AMT tax. To indicate this information to the IRS computer, you enter zero (-0-) on the AMT line on page 2 of Form 1040.

If your regular tax is *less than* the tentative AMT amount (on line 6 in Figure 11.3), **the difference** is your AMT tax. This amount becomes a direct add-on to your regular tax. When the two are added together, you get an *enhanced* tax. With AMT, therefore, your regular tax is automatically increased.

12

YOUR DEPENDENTS' RETURNS

> Every PRIMARY FILER Is Responsible For Assuring That Income Tax Returns, When Required, Are Prepared For, Or By, His Dependents. When Claiming A Dependent On The Primary Filer's Return, Care Is Required To Assure That The Dependent Does NOT Claim For Himself The Statutory Exemption Amount. To Avoid Any "Double Exemption" Claim, A Computational WORKSHEET Is Provided In The Instructions To Forms 1040EZ, 1040A, And 1040. Disabled And Older Family Members Who Are Not Money Dependent On The Primary Filer Often Become DEPENDENTS-IN-FACT For Return Filing Purposes.

As a parent (whether single or married), you have a duty to oversee that your children, other dependents, and your own parents (your children's grandparents) prepare and file their own tax returns, when required. In some cases, this may mean doing each such return yourself. In other cases, this may mean being an instructor to those dependents who are cavalier about tax matters, but who can — and want to — do their own returns. Different family situations require different parental attentions. In general, though, your goal is to help close family members avoid ever being traumatized by the IRS and the U.S. tax system.

In the case of your own children (whether natural, adopted, or step-children), you have a special instructional role to perform. You need to be a counselor always at their side. Your attention will span their very first tax return until they become adults who are fully self-supporting and financially on their own. This will mean your keeping all records for them. Once self-supporting, your children are no longer your tax dependents.

As we view your duty situation, there are three categories of dependents' returns that you need to oversee. In Category I are your children whom you expect to reach self-supporting adulthood, at some point. In Category II are those dependents of adult age (any close family members) who are incapable of self support for reasons which are highly valid. In Category III are your own parents, whether they are qualified tax dependents of yours or not. As such persons get older, they tend to become forgetful, often are in pain or physically impaired, and have to struggle on reduced incomes. Paying their medical bills becomes a major concern.

In this chapter, therefore, we want to offer some guidance on how you can oversee your dependents' own tax returns. You must help your dependents realize that as their sources and types of income emerge, tax returns **will be** required. There is no escaping this, even when one is a qualified tax dependent. Because we have already addressed in the latter part of Chapter 9 the subject of children under age 14 having investment income, we will not cover those situations here. We are addressing strictly those dependents who are required to, or who choose to, file their own returns. Our premise is that your dependents have no dependents of their own. Our premise also is that in this era of high-tech computer processing of tax returns, much inhumaneness occurs. Sometimes this tax inhumaneness borders on cruelty and outright intimidation. The example that follows illustrates what we mean.

Notice from the IRS

Receiving a computer notice from the IRS about one's tax return can be an intimidating experience. It can be frightening to a young person, especially if such a person has filed only one "short form" tax return in his/her lifetime. Here's how terrifying such a notice can be to a young person.

The daughter of a single mother was a student who filed a 1996 return (Form 1040EZ) solely to get a $26 refund on her W-2 withholdings on $2,586. This amount is below the threshold for mandatory filing. In 1997 she earned approximately the same income. Even though $32 was withheld, she did not file in that year (1997). She turned 18 and received a $100,000 inheritance from her deceased father. She put $10,000 into a bank account and $90,000 into three mutual funds managed by the same bank. She did not need the $32 refund for schooling purposes.

In June 1999, the IRS sent the 20-year-old daughter the following notice:

REQUEST FOR YOUR TAX RETURN. Our records show that we have not received your tax return (Form 1040) for the period ending 12-31-1997. . . . Our records indicate that you sold stock during the calendar year 1997. Please read the instructions for reporting this transaction on Form 1040, Schedule D, Capital Gains and Losses.

Not having ever filed a Form 1040, and not knowing what a Schedule D was, she did nothing. She was attending junior college full time, and was working on weekends.

Two months later (August 1999), the IRS contacted her again. This time the computer notice read:

YOUR TAX RETURN [FOR 1997] *IS OVERDUE. Please contact us immediately, or we may have to take the following actions:*

1. *Summon you to bring us your books and records.*
2. *Begin **criminal proceedings** which may include a fine, **imprisonment**, or both . . .*
3. *Prepare a tax bill for you . . . then begin **collection proceedings** such as filing a lien and **seizing your wages, other income**, property, and assets.* [Emphasis added.]

When you were 20 years old, how would **you** have reacted to this IRS heavy handedness?

At this point, the student became terrified and despondent . . . almost suicidal. She suffered many sleepless nights worrying about being put in jail. Concerned about her daughter's mental state, the mother contacted a tax person and directed that her daughter go see him for preparing the 1997 return.

Within a few days, a 1997 tax return was prepared showing a tax amount of $437. Since $32 already had been withheld, her actual tax due was $405. And for this, the IRS was going to commence "criminal proceedings"!

Worse yet, the State of California, where the above student resided, sent the following computer notice:

*FINAL NOTICE. Balance PAST DUE $3,636. We intend to take collection action without further notification if you do not immediately pay the above balance due in full. **Partial payment will not stop collection action.***

Subsequently, a California return was filed showing a tax due of $44 . . . NOT $3,636!

Behind the Notice(s)

Ordinarily, the IRS does not threaten criminal proceedings and imprisonment on $405 tax due. Nor does California ordinarily assert $3,636 when only $44 is due. What was behind these notices that made the tax collectors so tyrannical?

When the 20-year-old student received her $100,000 inheritance (at age 18), she left home and got her own apartment. On three separate occasions in 1997, she withdrew from her mutual funds a total of $32,000. Some of this was switched to other accounts, and some was used to pay rent, buy food, and pay other living expenses. Nevertheless, the entire $32,000 was reported to the IRS as "other income" (meaning: other than her $2,600 in W-2 wages). As a consequence, the IRS and the State of California were taxing her gross sales proceeds as ordinary W-2 income.

In actuality, the income (dividends and capital gains) that derived from her $90,000 in mutual funds came to about $8,000. This amount plus her $2,600 in W-2 earnings put her over the mandatory threshold for tax filing. Instead of $10,600 of income ($8,000 + $2,600) which she correctly reported, the IRS and California computers saw $42,600 ($10,600 + $32,000). The computers went on automatic. The collection threats went out fast and furious. No one in the IRS, nor the State, raised a finger to learn the true story.

Very few young people and elderly persons, and not all persons working full time, are aware that the IRS is privy to every financial transaction that one makes. Any money that goes through a licensed agent, broker, or financial institution is reported electronically to the IRS. The IRS, in turn, reports it electronically to state taxing agencies. Presto. At the touch of a key, the tax collection process begins. No agency human being ever intercedes. It is up to the taxpayer to pay, file, explain, or protest.

In the case above, the 20-year-old student suffered miserably and painfully. She received no guidance from her grieving mother (who had recently lost her husband), nor from anyone else among her family and friends. Such is the penalty that many dependents face from the marvels of the paperless, humanless cyberspace.

Guidelines for Oversight

The above is just one illustration of what can happen when you leave a dependent on his or her own. It's a tough tax world out there. Totally shielding a dependent against tax reality is NOT the goal. As a parent, your oversight goal is to *ease* your dependents into a tax system that will persist throughout their adult lives.

As a guideline for oversight measures on your part, we present Figure 12.1. The idea behind this figure is to categorize your dependents into income *types* (not amounts), age groupings, and dependency phaseout likelihood. Note that we show only eight income categories instead of the 15 income lines listed on Form 1040. We do so because, as your dependents, such persons are unlikely to be involved in complex income situations. Also note in Figure 12.1 that we show six age categories. By the time your children reach age 24, they should be self supporting. There are exceptions, of course, for those who are incapable of self support, unemployed, disabled, or who have special physical and psychological needs.

One reality you may face is that as your own parent(s) get increasingly older, they may become dependents-in-fact. That is,

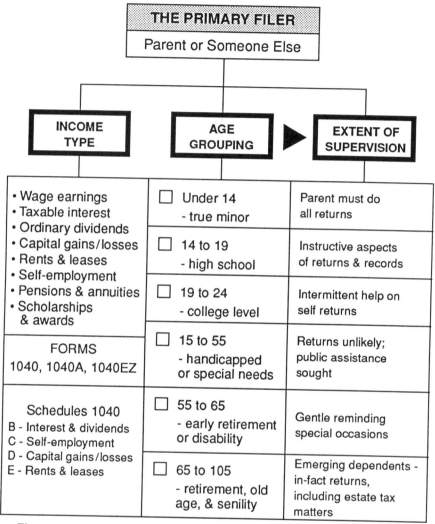

THE PRIMARY FILER		
Parent or Someone Else		
INCOME TYPE	**AGE GROUPING**	**EXTENT OF SUPERVISION**

• Wage earnings
• Taxable interest
• Ordinary dividends
• Capital gains/losses
• Rents & leases
• Self-employment
• Pensions & annuities
• Scholarships
  & awards
	☐ Under 14
	  - true minor
		Parent must do
		all returns

	☐ 14 to 19 - high school	Instructive aspects of returns & records
	☐ 19 to 24 - college level	Intermittent help on self returns

FORMS
1040, 1040A, 1040EZ
	☐ 15 to 55
	  - handicapped
	  or special needs
		Returns unlikely;
		public assistance
		sought

Schedules 1040
B - Interest & dividends
C - Self-employment
D - Capital gains/losses
E - Rents & leases
	☐ 55 to 65
	  - early retirement
	  or disability
		Gentle reminding
		special occasions

	☐ 65 to 105
	  - retirement, old
	  age, & senility
		Emerging dependents -
		in-fact returns,
		including estate tax
		matters

Fig. 12.1 - Classification Guidelines for Tax Supervision of Dependents

because of their retirement income, including social security, you may not be able to claim them as dependents on your own tax return. Nevertheless, because of their age, senility, poor health, loneliness, etc., you will probably have to do their tax returns for them, and monitor their financial resources.

In all cases, if the amount of tax accountable income by a dependent is a specified threshold amount (which changes each year), the filing of a federal return is required. The filing amount is based on a standard deduction plus personal exemption for each filing person. As the primary family filer, you'd like to preserve the personal exemption for each of your dependents for yourself. Therefore, for general oversight guidance, you need only think in terms of the "standard deduction." As a rough rule of thumb in this regard, use $5,000 as a target figure. For any combination of income, whether taxable or not, that exceeds $5,000, a tax return most likely will be required.

Caution: We use the term "rough rule of thumb." The $5,000 threshold amount is not official. For each dependent and each income category, always check the official instructions for the threshold amounts. For example, if one of your children is a student (in high school, college, or other training institution) and works as an *independent contractor* part time, he/she is considered self-employed. As such, a federal return is required when the net earnings (gross minus expenses) become $400 or more. This is the threshold for social security and medicare taxes.

For example, suppose a student earned $2,516 in self-employment income while attending junior college. There would be no income tax, as this amount is below the standard deduction ($4,700 in 2002) for earned income. However, as a self-employed person, the social security/medicare tax would be $385 ($2,516 x 15.3%). The social security/medicare tax is an entirely separate tax from the income tax. In other words: *two* taxes. As a consequence, self-employed dependents cannot use any of the "short" tax forms: 1040EZ, 1040A, or TeleFile.

Form 1040EZ & TeleFiling

For a dependent (student or otherwise) who works part time and derives less than $400 interest from a savings account, Form 1040EZ is ideal. Whether single or married, a 1040EZ is really a simple, simple return. Yet, think of it as a responsibility training tool for young dependents. It is applicable where there are only three income sources, namely:

1. Wages, salaries, and tips in box 1 of Form(s) W-2 _____
2. Taxable interest, not over $400 _____
3. Unemployment compensation _____

The total of these three items constitutes the dependent's AGI (Adjusted Gross Income).

Form 1040EZ is simple in another respect. On the back side thereof is a *Worksheet for dependents who checked "Yes" on line 5* [on the front]. The "line 5" reads—

Can your parents (or someone else) claim you on their return?

☐ *Yes. Enter amount from worksheet on back.*

The worksheet first applies the standard deduction, for single or married, then addresses the exemption amount. The exemption amount line reads—

- If single, enter 0.   }
- If married and—   }
  — both you and your spouse can be   } _____
     claimed as dependents, enter 0   }
- — only one of you can be claimed as   }
     a dependent, enter 3,000 [for 2002]   }

We think you should photocopy and keep this worksheet at your side, at all times. It will come in handy should the IRS dispute your claiming an exemption amount for one or more dependents who file separate tax returns from you. We present this worksheet to you in Figure 12.2. Note that the standard deduction and exemption amount are two different items, each with its own dollar amounts.

If Form 1040EZ is prepared correctly and filed on time, your dependent will be sent a TeleFile package the following year. The IRS has done an excellent job in simplifying its TeleFile instructions. They appear in a 20-page package titled:

___(year)___ *TeleFile, Tax Record and Instructions.*
Replaces your Form 1040EZ. 2 Easy Steps to File by Phone (toll free).

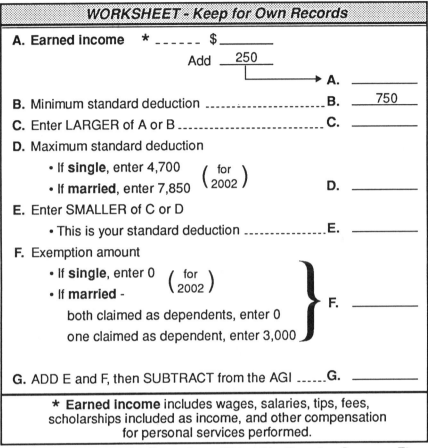

WORKSHEET - Keep for Own Records

A. Earned income   * _ _ _ _ _ _ $ _____

                Add   __250__

                             → A. _____

B. Minimum standard deduction _ _ _ _ _ _ _ _ _ _ B. __750__

C. Enter LARGER of A or B _ _ _ _ _ _ _ _ _ _ _ _ C. _____

D. Maximum standard deduction

     • If **single**, enter 4,700   (for)

     • If **married**, enter 7,850   (2002)   D. _____

E. Enter SMALLER of C or D

     • This is your standard deduction _ _ _ _ _ _ _ E. _____

F. Exemption amount

     • If **single**, enter 0   (for)

     • If **married** -   (2002)

         both claimed as dependents, enter 0   F. _____

         one claimed as dependent, enter 3,000

G. ADD E and F, then SUBTRACT from the AGI _ _ _ _ G. _____

* Earned income includes wages, salaries, tips, fees, scholarships included as income, and other compensation for personal services performed.

Fig. 12.2 - Worksheet for Dependents Claimed by Parent or Someone Else

In the instructions "Who Can File by Phone," it is not clear whether a parent or someone else claiming a dependent can file by phone for that dependent. The instructions use the term "you": meaning the telefiler. Since no signature is required on a telefiled return (your dependent's signature is on Form 1040EZ), and as long as you have all of the information necessary for telefiling, the IRS will most likely accept your telefiling on behalf of your dependent. Otherwise, Form 1040EZ **and** telefiling present excellent opportunities for tax training your dependents. Such is also an opportunity for you to gauge the tax temperament and record-keeping discipline of each of your dependents. They might as well get used to income taxes and recordkeeping, early on. Once they start having to file, they will have to do so well into retirement and old age. Taxes are forever!

Form 1040A More Versatile

Form 1040A is midway between the simplicity of Form 1040EZ and the comprehensiveness of Form 1040. Whereas 1040EZ accommodates only three sources of income, Form 1040A accommodates up to eight sources. These eight sources are:

1. Wages, salaries, tips, etc.
2. Taxable interest
3. Ordinary dividends
4. Capital gain distributions
5. IRA withdrawals
6. Pensions and annuities
7. Unemployment compensation
8. Social security benefits

When these items, as applicable, are added, the result constitutes your dependent's total income.

In addition to more versatility in types of income, Form 1040A also permits two adjustments to income. The two adjustments are:

- IRA deduction
- Student loan interest deduction

From the above listed items, the usefulness of Form 1040A would be apparent for dependents who are—

- Working students, single mostly, who are contributing to or withdrawing from IRA accounts.
- Young marrieds, both of whom are working (off and on), both of whom are students, one of whom is working and one a student, or one working and one unemployed.
- Elderly/blind persons, single or married, one or both over 65, one or both blind (20/200 or more in the better eye).

When your dependent gets to the standard deduction part of Form 1040A, it says—

See page _____ [of instructions] *if someone can claim you as a dependent.*

This instruction directs you to a **Standard Deduction Worksheet for Dependents**. This worksheet is similar in format to Figure 12.2 but with the complication of an elderly/blind *additional* standard deduction. The additional standard deduction is $1,000 for a single elderly/blind and $1,800 for married elderly/blind. These additional amounts are indexed for inflation from year to year.

When Form 1040 Required

Neither 1040EZ nor 1040A can be used when there are itemized deductions (Schedule A), self-employment income (Schedule C), capital gains or losses (Schedule D), or rental property income (Schedule E). If any one of these four schedules applies to any of your dependents, Form 1040 must be used. Not doing so can lead to the computer tyranny problems that we cited earlier for a 20-year-old junior college student.

Student dependents of any age up to 24 are unlikely to have a need for Schedule A (1040): **Itemized Deductions** (medical expenses, property taxes, home mortgage interest, charitable gifts, etc.) This schedule is more likely to be used by elderly, blind, or disabled dependents. The likelihood here, though, is that, in order to benefit from Schedule A, the dependent has to show a total income that at least equals the amount of Schedule A deductions claimed. Such an amount of income by the dependent may disqualify you from the dependency exemption, under the support test discussed back in Chapter 2.

Here's an example of what we mean. You have an elderly parent whom you have been claiming as a dependent. Your parent has Schedule A deductions of $10,000. (For simplicity, assume the standard deduction to be $5,000.) In order to use Schedule A, your parent needs to have a tax accountable income of at least $10,000. At this level, you need to show that you contributed $10,001 or more towards your parent's support. If you do so, your claim to the dependency exemption will stand. But if you contribute only $6,000, say, you will lose the exemption for that parent.

Incidentally, both the 1040A and the 1040 carry this instruction at the first exemption checkbox on each form:

> *If your parent (or someone else) can claim you as a dependent on his or her tax return,* **do not check** *[this] box* ☐.

Then, at the standard deduction line, your dependent is instructed as follows:

> *Enter the* **larger** *of* [the] *standard deduction shown below . . . OR* [the] *itemized deductions from Schedule A.*

Either way, no exemption is claimed by your dependent for himself/herself (because you, the primary filer, are claiming the exemption).

In our view, the most versatile use of Form 1040 is by a serious-minded student in college. So long as your dependent who is a student is enrolled full time for any five months of an academic year, and is under 24 years of age, he/she can qualify as your dependent. As a student, one is not required to consume all income for self support. A qualified student may save his otherwise consumable income to launch a career after all schooling is complete. This makes it easier for a parent (or someone else) to qualify under the more-than-50% total support test.

A serious-minded student in college often has been blessed with gifts and inheritances over the years (since birth) from parents, grandparents, uncles, aunts, and, perhaps, others. Such a student may find that, while Schedule A is not applicable, other 1040 Schedules are applicable. Such a student may be working part time, may be self-employed now and then, keeps track of his investments, and/or collects rent from property which was acquired by inheritance. The "tax profile" of such a student might evolve along the lines that we present in Figure 12.3. The message being presented is that there is nothing improper about a student having comfortable income, so long as his/her curriculum of studies is pursued conscientiously.

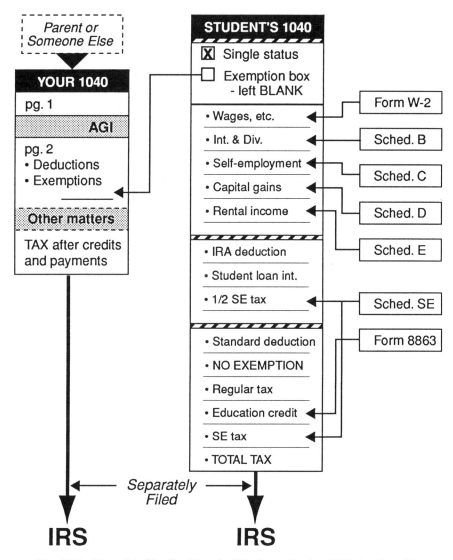

Fig. 12.3 - Plausible Tax Profile of a "Serious Student" Under Age 24

Assigning Assets to Minors

As a parent (or someone else), once you become acclimated to preparing a dependent's return — or supervising its preparation — various family strategies open up. By one simple technique alone, you can *dilute* your (and your spouse's) total income. You can do this dilution by transferring, gratuitously, **income-producing assets** to one or more of your minor children. Here, we use the term "minor" with reference to the legal age of a dependent in the state where you and your dependent reside. For most states, one's legal age is 18. By assigning assets to a minor — gradually over many years — you are setting the stage for that minor to become self-supporting by the time the minor completes schooling, starts working full time, or gets married.

You cannot assign your own income to a minor, nor to anyone else, in order to reduce your tax. But you can assign assets, which themselves generate income. Once an income-producing asset is assigned to a minor and the ownership thereto properly noted, any subsequent income is taxable to the assignee.

The most practical assets for income dilution purposes are stocks, bonds, mutual fund shares, installment notes, mineral rights, rental property (real and tangible), and other items (such as land) that can be expected to appreciate in value over time. In the assignment process, make sure that the asset is retitled in the *name* and *SSN* (social security number) of the assignee. When a minor is a designated owner of an income-producing asset, the custodian of that asset will insist that the parent's name (or guardian's name) also be used. In this case, ownership of the asset should be indicated as:

_____(name of minor)___   Soc. Sec. No._____
c/o___(parent's name)___ or ____(guardian's name)_____

Some asset custodians such as banks and brokerage institutions will insist that a minor's account be identified with *your* SSN. If your child is age 14 or over, resist doing so, vehemently. Otherwise, if listed in your SSN, the IRS computer will attack you for failing to report the income. The IRS will do this, even though you may have already reported the income under the minor's SSN and paid tax on it. If you encounter an adamant custodian who won't listen to reason, change the account to another custodial institution and enter the minor's SSN as though it were your own.

When it comes time to prepare a minor's return with asset-derived income, be mindful that you have to use Form 1040. This is because asset-produced income goes on Schedules B (interest and dividends), D (capital gains and losses), and E (supplemental income). Recall Figure 12.3.

When preparing the 1040 and submitting it to the IRS, make sure that the minor can sign his or her name *legibly*. If a minor cannot sign a return legibly because of injury, handicap, or other reason, the IRS's instructions say—

> *Either parent may sign the child's name in the space provided. Then add "By (your signature), as parent* [or guardian] *for minor child."*

Employing Your Children

If you have a trade, business, or profession where you engage one or more employees, another strategizing opportunity presents itself. As the owner or co-owner of a business, engage your own children. There is nothing improper about this if you do it right. "Doing it right" means treating your children like any other employee working on your business premises. That is, while your children are on your premises, think of them as essential persons for making your business a success.

"Doing it right" means assigning your children bona fide tasks which are *ordinary and necessary* for the type of business you have. Provide them with a written job description, and set an hourly rate comparable to (though slightly *lower* than) that paid to nonfamily employees for the same tasks. Just like your nonfamily employees, your children receive a paycheck subject to withholdings. If your children are first-time employees for you or anyone else, expect static from them on the withholdings. They'll argue with you as their parent that the withholdings are "not fair." The withholding experience becomes their first wake-up call to the real world: Tax Life, USA. The point is driven home when you inform your children that the withholding of social security/ medicare tax is NOT refundable.

Use common sense. Do **not** employ your children who are under 14 years of age. Aside from transgressing child labor laws, a person of this age rarely takes assigned tasks seriously. Wait until your children are in high school, when there's a need for extra spending money. When such need arises, your children will be more receptive to working for you (or for someone else) part time. Should a child of yours become a high school dropout or a disciplinary problem for school administrators, employing such a child in your business may help in the re-orientation process. Some teenagers have to learn the hard way about the importance of education in their approaching adult life.

As a rule of thumb, limit the gross pay to your children to $5,000 (approximately) per year. This way, only a minimum amount of income tax (approximately $100) is required to be withheld. Correspondingly, about $385 in social security/medicare tax would be withheld. The withholding experience itself is good training for your children. If you pay them more than $5,000, you run the risk of losing them as a dependent on your own tax return.

Dependent-in-Fact I

Earlier, we mentioned the possibility of a family member having to file a tax return for an older family member who is not financially dependent upon the filer. This is what we call: *Nominee filing* for a dependent-in-fact. The "nominee filer" is the family member having regular contact with the person who cannot file on his own. No particular legal formality is required, so long as the nominee files a required return properly. We illustrate the point with two recent — and contrasting — real-life examples.

In Example I, the parents were divorced and lived separately. The youngest daughter was attending college near where her father lived. As he was in poor health, she visited him several times a week. He died in 1989 when the daugher was 23 years old. He had filed his own return for 1988. Not knowing what to do for 1989, the daughter did nothing.

Six years later, in March 1995, the daughter was served with a *Notice of Federal Tax Lien* for $4,228. This amount included penalties, interest, and statutory additions. Apparently, her sick father had overlooked reporting a small amount of income for 1988. Again, not knowing what to do, the daughter did nothing. She was not responsible for her father's taxes, she reasoned.

For the next three years (1995 through 1998), the IRS became more hostile, egregious, and threatening with its computer demands. She tried numerous times to contact the IRS to explain the situation, but she got nowhere. Finally, in December 1998, at the behest of friends, she contacted a tax preparer.

With the aid of the tax preparer, she wrote the following letter to the IRS District Director:

I am unmarried and did not know what to do when my father died. I had no experience in tax matters. Every time I contacted your office for help, I was scolded, reprimanded, and threatened with more penalties. One of your employees actually screamed at me over the phone. This upset me to the point where I failed several of my classes, and had to drop out of college for a time. The lien has prevented me from getting any student loans.

I am so distraught over this matter that I am sending a copy of this letter to my Congressman and to the Commissioner of the IRS. I am asking them to be helpful and humane, instead of threatening me the way you have been doing.

/s/_____
For the Estate of_____

After **seven** phone contacts between the tax preparer and the IRS, there was issued a—

Certificate of Non-Attachment of Federal Tax Lien

The reason for this action is that it has been determined that ____[the daughter]____ is not liable for the tax under the above assessment.

/s/_____
District Director, IRS

Dependent-in-Fact II

In our real-life Example II, a 67-year-old niece was tax responsible for filing her aunt's tax returns. At age 96, the aunt had a massive stroke and was hospitalized. Upon release from the hospital, she went directly into a full-care nursing home. There she remained until reaching the age of 104 . . . when she died. Death occurred in 1998.

The 67-year-old niece (who had turned age 75) prepared and filed her aunt's income tax returns for years 1991 through 1998. In 1998, the aunt's total income (including the taxable portion of social security) came to about $42,000. For the same year, her nursing home expenses totaled $57,800. This meant that there was no income tax to pay. Actually, there was no or negligible income tax to pay for all eight of the nursing home years.

Upon the aunt's death, her 75-year-old niece was appointed executor. This meant that she had to prepare and file a death tax return. This is IRS Form 706: *U.S. Estate Tax Return*. Form 706 is a 44-page return, although in this case only 12 pages were required. Upon completing Form 706, the aunt's death taxable estate turned out to be approximately $1,400,000. Of this amount, a total of $198,000 had to be paid as death tax ($140,000 to the IRS and $58,000 to the State of California). This left approximately $1,202,000 (1,400,000 − 198,000) to be distributed to the four heirs (or about $300,000 to each).

Who do you think was responsible for paying the death tax?

Answer: the executor — the 75-year-old niece. On this matter, Section 2002 of the Internal Revenue Code: *Liability for Payment*, says quite succinctly—

The tax imposed [as estate tax] *shall be paid by the executor.*

What is the moral here?

It is that, in a family situation, someone is always responsible for preparing or supervising the preparation of a family member's tax return. This holds true from birth to death. It makes little difference whether a parent (or someone else) does so for his own dependents or for his dependents-in-fact. The reality is: Revenue for Government must go on from generation to generation . . . on down family lines.

ABOUT

THE AUTHOR

Holmes F. Crouch

Born on a small farm in southern Maryland, Holmes was graduated from the U.S. Coast Guard Academy with a Bachelor's Degree in Marine Engineering. While serving on active duty, he wrote many technical articles on maritime matters. After attaining the rank of Lieutenant Commander, he resigned to pursue a career as a nuclear engineer.

Continuing his education, he earned a Master's Degree in Nuclear Engineering from the University of California. He also authored two books on nuclear propulsion. As a result of the tax write-offs associated with writing these books, the IRS audited his returns. The IRS's handling of the audit procedure so annoyed Holmes that he undertook to become as knowledgeable as possible regarding tax procedures. He became a licensed private Tax Practitioner by passing an examination administered by the IRS. Having attained this credential, he started his own tax preparation and counseling business in 1972.

In the early years of his tax practice, he was a regular talk-show guest on San Francisco's KGO Radio responding to hundreds of phone-in tax questions from listeners. He was a much sought-after guest speaker at many business seminars and taxpayer meetings. He also provided counseling on special tax problems, such as divorce matters, property exchanges, timber harvesting, mining ventures, animal breeding, independent contractors, selling businesses, and offices-at-home. Over the past 25 years, he has prepared nearly 10,000 tax returns for individuals, estates, trusts, and small businesses (in partnership and corporate form).

During the tax season of January through April, he prepares returns in a unique manner. During a single meeting, he completes the return . . . *on the spot!* The client leaves with his return signed, sealed, and in a stamped envelope. His unique approach to preparing returns and his personal interest in his clients' tax affairs have honed his professional proficiency. His expertise extends through itemized deductions, computer-matching of income sources, capital gains and losses, business expenses and cost of goods, residential rental expenses, limited and general partnership activities, closely-held corporations, to family farms and ranches.

He remembers spending 12 straight hours completing a doctor's complex return. The next year, the doctor, having moved away, utilized a large accounting firm to prepare his return. Their accountant was so impressed by the manner in which the prior return was prepared that he recommended the doctor travel the 500 miles each year to have Holmes continue doing it.

He recalls preparing a return for an unemployed welder, for which he charged no fee. Two years later the welder came back and had his return prepared. He paid the regular fee . . . and then added a $300 tip.

During the off season, he represents clients at IRS audits and appeals. In one case a shoe salesman's audit was scheduled to last three hours. However, after examining Holmes' documentation it was concluded in 15 minutes with "no change" to his return. In another instance he went to an audit of a custom jeweler that the IRS dragged out for more than six hours. But, supported by Holmes' documentation, the client's return was accepted by the IRS with "no change."

Then there was the audit of a language translator that lasted two full days. The auditor scrutinized more than $1.25 million in gross receipts, all direct costs, and operating expenses. Even though all expensed items were documented and verified, the auditor decided that more than $23,000 of expenses ought to be listed as capital items for depreciation instead. If this had been enforced it would have resulted in a significant additional amount of tax. Holmes strongly disagreed and after many hours of explanation got the amount reduced by more than 60% on behalf of his client.

He has dealt extensively with gift, death and trust tax returns. These preparations have involved him in the tax aspects of wills, estate planning, trustee duties, probate, marital and charitable bequests, gift and death exemptions, and property titling.

Although not an attorney, he prepares Petitions to the U.S. Tax Court for clients. He details the IRS errors and taxpayer facts by citing pertinent sections of tax law and regulations. In a recent case involving an attorney's ex-spouse, the IRS asserted a tax deficiency of $155,000. On behalf of his client, he petitioned the Tax Court and within six months the IRS conceded the case.

Over the years, Holmes has observed that the IRS is not the industrious, impartial, and competent federal agency that its official public imaging would have us believe.

He found that, at times, under the slightest pretext, the IRS has interpreted against a taxpayer in order to assess maximum penalties, and may even delay pending matters so as to increase interest due on additional taxes. He has confronted the IRS in his own behalf on five separate occasions, going before the U.S. Claims Court, U.S. District Court, and U.S. Tax Court. These were court actions that tested specific sections of the Internal Revenue Code which he found ambiguous, inequitable, and abusively interpreted by the IRS.

Disturbed by the conduct of the IRS and by the general lack of tax knowledge by most individuals, he began an innovative series of taxpayer-oriented Federal tax guides. To fulfill this need, he undertook the writing of a series of guidebooks that provide in-depth knowledge on one tax subject at a time. He focuses on subjects that plague taxpayers all throughout the year. Hence, his formulation of the "Allyear" Tax Guide series.

The author is indebted to his wife, Irma Jean, and daughter, Barbara MacRae, for the word processing and computer graphics that turn his experiences into the reality of these publications. Holmes welcomes comments, questions, and suggestions from his readers. He can be contacted in California at (408) 867-2628, or by writing to the publisher's address.

ALLYEAR Tax Guides
by Holmes F. Crouch